Barbecue

THE AUSTRALIAN
Women's Weekly

Barbecue

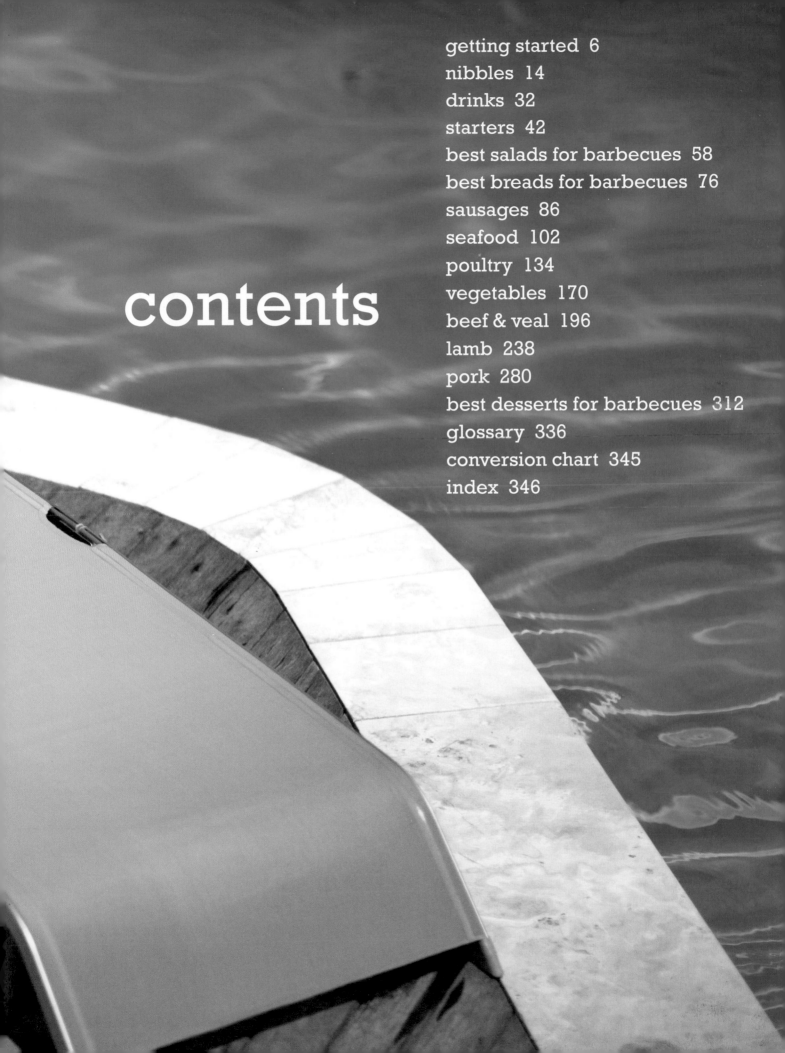

contents

There is something almost therapeutic about collecting friends and family around the barbecue, slowly cooking the meat, settling to a table dressed with simple, tasty salads and delicious barbecued meat and vegies. Yes, the barbecue needs no introduction – it's an Aussie institution we all know and love. But are we making the most of this humble contraption? Without too much fuss, you can break away from the snags and steaks you're used to, and start cooking something a little more special. Add some spark to your sizzle with the recipes and tips in this book.

getting started

which barbecue
is for you?

Indispensable barbecue accessories

Disposable baking dish
Meat thermometer
Bamboo skewers
Basting brush
Long-handled tongs
Wire brush and a metal scraper
Fish grill
PVC polyester barbecue cover

When choosing which barbecue is best for you, consider whether you want the option to cook big joints of meat using a barbecue with indirect heat, or whether you'll only use your barbecue for more quickly grilled steaks and sausages over direct heat. Choose a barbecue based on what size is suitable, whether you'll need it to be portable, and which fuel you want to use.

Size

Trolley barbecues, though essentially portable, are generally set up as a permanent or semi-permanent unit. There is an enormous variety of accessories available and they come with two, four, six or even eight burners. Four burners are usually enough for most requirements.

Kettle barbecues, such as the Weber, are more portable and are best known for using charcoal or briquettes – giving you the option of cooking with either direct or indirect heat. When set up for direct heat, the barbecue works wonderfully for simple grilling; and when set up for indirect heat, it is perfect for smoking and roasting a succulent, barbecued whole bird, ham or roast.

Hibachi or simple cooking grills are very versatile, portable barbecues.

Fuel

Gas is a comfortable compromise between convenience and flavour. Gas is cheap and readily available, easy-to-use and heats the barbecue quickly. It also makes less mess than other fuel types, such as briquettes (heat beads) and charcoal, most commonly used on kettle barbecues. Charcoal, while producing a brilliant smoky flavour, can be a labour of love as it takes a long time to heat up and can be hard to get going. To light the coals you need fire starters and both these and the charcoal are expensive, and you'll need to buy fresh ones regularly.

Wood barbecues are wonderful for smoking, where the flavours of food are affected by the choice of wood used. Never use treated wood and always check that you are allowed to burn wood in your neighbourhood. For an excellent alternative, try using a smoke box filled with wood chips – available from barbecue retailers.

Electric-fuelled barbecues are generally accepted as a weak alternative to the previous fuel options, but are becoming more popular for small spaces. They are cheap to run, but don't get very hot.

Grill material

Cast iron is the most popular grill plate material – it is cheap, easy to clean and a great conductor of heat.

Stainless steel hotplates are considerably more durable and are more hygienic than cast iron, which is a porous metal. However, they are very expensive, do not conduct heat as well and require careful cleaning. Certain oils, in particular, olive oil, are nearly impossible to clean off.

Enamel coated hotplates are similar to cast iron and are scratch-proof.

Tools of the trade

Trolley barbecues come with a variety of features. An important one is a hood or cover, which doubles the versatility of your barbecue by allowing you to use it as an oven. The hood usually comes with a temperature gauge, which removes the guesswork when a certain cooking temperature is called for. The hotplate is a flat cooking surface perfect for fried onions, vegies and burgers. It often makes up half of the surface area of a barbecue. A rotisserie is also a very popular addition. It is attached to a power outlet and rotates large cuts of meat above the surface for an even, long, slow roast. As as the name suggests, a wok burner allows a wok to sit neatly over the gas heat source enabling you to stir-fry outdoors, or even make a sauce to accompany your meat.

Before you start

Before you start cooking on a new barbecue, you must season or cure the grill. This helps with cleaning later on, and burns off the residual chemicals left on the grill from the manufacturing process.

1. Give your cast iron grill and hotplates a good scrub with warm soapy water and dry thoroughly.

2. Lightly spray all over with canola oil spray. Some manufacturers advise against using aerosol sprays on their products; check the instructions that come with the barbecue. If this is the case, use some newspaper to brush oil over the grill.

3. Put the cast iron grill and hotplates in place on the barbecue and, with the hood open, heat it on high until the cast iron begins to smoke, then reduce the heat to low.

4. Use a metal barbecue brush to scrub the grill, repeatedly dipping the brush in water. Some of the black coating will lift off – this is perfectly normal and nothing to worry about.

5. Cool the barbecue and cast iron plates and repeat the process.

6. Finish with another spray, or wipe, all over with canola oil.

Fire it up

Just before heating, brush or spray both food and barbecue with melted butter or oil. When heating a gas barbecue, 10 to 15 minutes should be enough. A wood or charcoal barbecue, however, could take up to an hour to be properly hot.

If using a kettle barbecue, set up the coals for indirect heat or direct heat, as required, after the coals are hot. For indirect heat, move coals to the outside edges of the barbecue and cook food in the centre. Use a disposable baking dish nestled in the coals to catch drips. Don't cook anything while the fire starters are burning or the only infused flavour you'll taste will be kerosene.

Ensure the barbecue is at the temperature required by the recipe before adding the food. A good heat test is to see how long you can hold your hand just above the surface of the grill. It is a very hot fire if you can hold your hand in place for one second or less, three seconds for a medium-hot barbecue, and five seconds for a low-medium fire.

Direct heat cooking

Don't prick sausages before cooking them as this simply allows the moisture to leak out, leaving them dry and tasteless. Sausages should take a long time to cook over a low heat; if they look like they are about to burst, move them to a cooler part of the barbecue. For nicely char-marked steaks, grill them for a few minutes without moving and turn once only so that the marks will be clearly defined.

Baste food frequently with more butter or oil (or with a marinade or sauce according to the recipe). Cook thin or delicate items on one side until well marked; turn and cook a further minute or less and serve marked-side up. Cooking times suggested in this book are a guide only, so test the meat before the suggested cooking time is complete. Don't cut the meat to test for doneness, as this will release all the precious juices that make it tender, moist and flavoursome. Instead, press on the surface of the meat with your tongs. For rare, it will be soft to the touch; for medium it will be firm; and for well-done it will be very firm. Seafood should be removed from the barbecue while it is still a shade underdone; its own heat will finish cooking it by the time it is served. Fillets of fish are too delicate to cook on a barbecue and should either be wrapped in, or cooked on, aluminium foil. Baste once or twice with the juices and cook only for about 4 minutes for fillets, and 7 minutes for thick steaks.

cooking techniques

Indirect heat cooking

Indirect heat is great for cooking large joints of meat, such as a ham, large roast or whole bird – which comes in handy if you're serving a crowd. Follow the manufacturer's guidelines to heat the barbecue to the required temperature. To cook, place the meat on a wire rack in a disposable baking tray. Frequent basting will keep the meat moist and create a deliciously sticky glaze. Test for doneness by inserting a skewer into the meat. For rare meat, the juices should run red; if the juices are pink, the meat is cooked medium-rare; and if the juices are clear, the meat is well-done.

Poultry is cooked only when the juices run without a trace of pink when a skewer is inserted into the fleshy parts of the bird. Protect wings or legs from burning by loosely covering them in aluminium foil. Test meat towards the end of the recommended cooking time and, if using a meat thermometer, leave it in the meat for a few minutes until the temperature stabilises.
For whole pieces of fish, handling is made much easier by using a fish grill. Slash the sides of the fish a few times before cooking. Fish is cooked when a skewer is inserted easily into its flesh. Remember to take it off the heat before it is completely cooked.
Rest all meat for an appropriate length of time before serving.

barbecue care

General

A gas bottle should be tested every 10 years, but aside from that, you need to keep up your own inspection and maintenance program. Barbecues often lie dormant in backyards over winter; during that time, disconnect the gas bottle from the barbecue. When it gets to barbecue season once again, check hoses for cracks or other damage and make sure connections are secure.

To check for gas leaks, make sure your gas bottle is full, all pipes are connected and the tank valve is in the ON position. Spray the pipes and connections slowly with soapy water and look for air bubbles. Even a small amount of gas will cause bubbles to form. If there are bubbles, turn off the gas and replace the connection or the hose.

Inspect cooking plates for rust and replace if necessary. Be prepared and check your barbecue before you plan to cook on it. The drip tray underneath the barbecue should be cleaned out regularly and sand or fat absorber replaced; apart from the obvious hygiene risk, leaving fat to accumulate here can cause flare ups when cooking.

Whenever the barbecue is not in use, protect it from the elements, and significantly prolong its life, by using a PVC polyester barbecue cover.

Cleaning

To prevent gas build-up in the hose when you have finished cooking on your gas barbecue, turn the heat up to high. When the plate starts to smoke, turn the gas off at the bottle, then at the controls.

To clean the barbecue plates, scrub the grill and plate with a stiff wire brush and cold water – not soapy. Wipe dry with some newspaper or an old towel. When the grill has cooled, spray or brush it with canola oil to prevent it rusting.

Clean a charcoal barbecue in the same way. When you have finished cleaning the grills and hotplates, allow the ash in the barbecue to cool, then place in a plastic bag and discard or sprinkle it over your garden.

Wipe the vents of kettle barbecues frequently to make sure they are clear and that air can flow freely through when open.

For the rest of the barbecue use a brass bristle brush to lightly clean off any excess build-up. If the barbecue still has remnants from the last time it was used, heat it and use a wire brush and warm water, not soapy, to scrape off any grime, then wipe it dry with a damp cloth.

A successful entertainer often uses the barbecue as an extension of the kitchen in summer. It is an informal, relaxing way to prepare the meal that allows you to mingle with your guests while you cook. To keep yourself as relaxed as your visitors, a little preparation goes a long way.

• Make accompaniments before the guests arrive. Salads can be assembled up until the point where the dressing is added, and roast vegies can be pre-prepared and kept warm in a very slow oven.
When the food on the barbecue is cooked, all the side dishes you prepared earlier can miraculously appear from the kitchen.

• Do not overload the barbecue. With manageable batches, the barbecue will keep a consistent heat, but if you load too much on, you could be standing over the barbecue all night. Keep the meat warm as you work by placing it on the warmer rack or cover it with foil and rest in a warm place such as a very slow oven.

• The golden rule in catering is to over-cater. Make sure there is at least enough food for there to be leftovers for you to eat the next day.

• When calculating how much to cook, make sure you take your guests into consideration – are they big or small eaters, and are they likely to devour the meat and pick at the vegies?

• A rule of thumb calculation for food quantities is to allow for about 200g uncooked meat per person – this quantity can be made up from a combination of red meat, chicken, and/or fish. Add a little more if you are using a cut of meat that includes the bone. In addition, there should be about a cup of carbohydrate, such as rice, pasta or potato salad, a cup of salad, and a roll and a half per person.

• Add a few phantom guests to your calculation and you will be sure to cover everyone. Add to that some of the nibbles from chapter one and a few starters from chapter three and you will have every guest happily full.

entertaining tips

nibbles

Fresh, light, palate-teasers prepare
the tastebuds for the char-grilled
flavours to come. Use skewers, large
leaves or toothpicks to make them
easy to eat with your hands.

grilled haloumi
with lemon

400g haloumi cheese, sliced thinly
9 pickled green chillies, drained
1 medium lemon (140g), cut into wedges

1 Cook cheese on heated oiled barbecue flat plate until browned.

2 Arrange cheese on platter; top with chillies and lemon wedges. Serve immediately, with olives and pitta bread, if desired.

preparation time 5 minutes
cooking time 5 minutes serves 8
nutritional count per serving 8.6g total fat
(5.5g saturated fat); 523kJ (125 cal);
1.1g carbohydrate; 10.8g protein; 0.4g fibre

basil dip

100g fresh basil leaves
⅔ cup (160ml) olive oil
1 clove garlic, quartered
2 teaspoons finely grated lemon rind
2 tablespoons finely grated parmesan cheese

1 Blend or process ingredients until smooth.

preparation time 5 minutes makes 1 cup
nutritional count per teaspoon 3.1g total fat
(0.5g saturated fat); 121kJ (29 cal);
0g carbohydrate; 0.2g protein; 0.1g fibre

olive dip

300g large black olives, seeded
2 tablespoons rinsed, drained capers
1 clove garlic, quartered
2 tablespoons lemon juice
1 tablespoon finely chopped fresh flat-leaf parsley
⅓ cup (80ml) olive oil

1 Blend or process ingredients until smooth.

preparation time 10 minutes makes 1½ cups
nutritional count per teaspoon 1.1g total fat
(0.2g saturated fat); 59kJ (14 cal);
1g carbohydrate; 0.0g protein; 0.1g fibre

anchovy dip

40 anchovy fillets, rinsed, drained
⅓ cup (80ml) olive oil
1 tablespoon lemon juice
2 cloves garlic, quartered
3 teaspoons fresh lemon thyme leaves
2 tablespoons boiling water

1 Blend or process anchovies, oil, juice, garlic and thyme until smooth.

2 Transfer to small bowl; stir in the boiling water.

preparation time 5 minutes makes 1 cup
nutritional count per teaspoon 1.8g total fat
(0.3g saturated fat); 84kJ (20 cal);
0g carbohydrate; 0.9g protein; 0g fibre

Serve the dips with fresh or lightly cooked vegetables, bread sticks or crackers.

from top: basil dip, olive dip, anchovy dip

fetta and olive dip with garlic toast

⅓ cup (40g) seeded green olives
200g soft fetta cheese
1 clove garlic, quartered
¾ cup (200g) yogurt
2 tablespoons finely chopped green olives
1 loaf ciabatta bread (440g)
2 tablespoons olive oil
2 cloves garlic, crushed

1 Blend or process whole olives, cheese, quartered garlic and yogurt until smooth. Transfer to small serving bowl; stir in chopped olives.

2 Cut bread into 18 slices. Brush bread with combined oil and crushed garlic; grill bread slices until browned both sides. Halve toasts diagonally; serve with dip.

preparation time *20 minutes*
cooking time *5 minutes* serves *6*
nutritional count per serving *17.9g total fat
(7.1g saturated fat); 1668kJ (399 cal);
43.3g carbohydrate; 14.3g protein; 3.1g fibre*

Dip can be kept, covered, in the refrigerator for up to one week.

dukkah

1 cup (150g) sesame seeds
⅓ cup (55g) whole blanched almonds
⅓ cup (50g) pistachios
⅓ cup ground coriander
¼ cup ground cumin
1 teaspoon salt
½ teaspoon freshly ground black pepper

1 Preheat oven to 220°C/200°C fan-forced.

2 Roast the sesame seeds, almonds and pistachios, separately, about 10 minutes or until browned lightly. Cool.

3 Blend or process nuts until fine; transfer to medium bowl. Add seeds, coriander, cumin, salt and pepper to nut mixture; mix well. Store in an airtight container.

preparation time *15 minutes*
cooking time *30 minutes* makes *about 2 cups*
nutritional count per tablespoon *5.8g total fat
(0.6g saturated fat); 272kJ (65 cal);
0.5g carbohydrate; 2.3g protein; 1g fibre*

Dukkah originated in Egypt; it is a blend of roasted nuts and spices. Serve the dukkah with a loaf of turkish or crusty bread, along with a bowl of extra virgin olive oil, for dipping bread. It is also delicious used as a crunchy coating for chicken or fish fillets.

fetta and olive dip with garlic toast

dukkah

mini scallop and lime kebabs

oysters with lime and coriander

mini scallop and lime kebabs

2 tablespoons vegetable oil
4cm piece fresh ginger (20g), grated
3 cloves garlic, crushed
24 scallops (600g), roe removed
3 limes
12 fresh kaffir lime leaves, halved lengthways
24 sturdy toothpicks

1 Combine oil, ginger and garlic in medium bowl; add scallops, toss to coat in marinade. Cover; refrigerate 30 minutes.

2 Cut each lime into eight wedges. Skewer one piece of lime leaf and one lime wedge onto each toothpick.

3 Cook scallops on heated oiled barbecue until cooked. Skewer one scallop onto each toothpick.

preparation time *15 minutes (plus refrigeration time)*
cooking time *5 minutes* makes *24*
nutritional count per kebab *1.7g total fat
(0.2g saturated fat); 121kJ (29 cal);
0.3g carbohydrate; 3g protein; 0.2g fibre*

oysters with lime and coriander

24 oysters, on the half shell
¼ cup (60ml) lime juice
1 teaspoon Tabasco sauce
2 tablespoons finely chopped fresh coriander
2 green onions, sliced thinly
1 tablespoon peanut oil
1 clove garlic, crushed
1 teaspoon brown sugar

1 Remove oysters from shells; wash and dry shells. Return oysters to shells; place on serving platter.

2 Combine remaining ingredients in screw-top jar; shake well. Divide dressing among oysters.

preparation time *10 minutes* makes *24*
nutritional count per oyster *1g total fat
(0.2g saturated fat); 67kJ (16 cal);
0.3g carbohydrate; 1.3g protein; 0.1g fibre*

Dressing can be made a day ahead; keep, covered, in the refrigerator.

oysters with mirin and wasabi

12 oysters, on the half shell
2 tablespoons mirin
1 tablespoon chinese cooking wine
1 tablespoon japanese soy sauce
½ teaspoon wasabi paste
1 green onion, chopped finely
¼ lebanese cucumber (30g), seeded, chopped finely

1 Remove oysters from shells; wash and dry shells. Return oysters to shells; place on serving platter.

2 Combine mirin, wine, sauce and paste in small saucepan; bring to the boil. Reduce heat; simmer dressing, uncovered, 2 minutes.

3 Divide warm dressing among oysters; top with combined green onion and cucumber.

preparation time *10 minutes*
cooking time *3 minutes* makes *12*
nutritional count per oyster *0.2g total fat
(0.1g saturated fat); 54kJ (13 cal);
0.3g carbohydrate; 1.4g protein; 0.1g fibre*

chicken caesar on baby cos leaves

2 slices day-old white bread (90g), crusts removed
2 slices prosciutto (30g)
1 cup (160g) shredded barbecued chicken
⅓ cup (80ml) caesar dressing
½ cup (40g) flaked parmesan cheese
2 baby cos lettuce (360g)

1 Cut bread into 1cm squares; toast bread until browned lightly all over.

2 Cook prosciutto on heated oiled barbecue until crisp. Drain on absorbent paper; chop coarsely.

3 Place croûtons and prosciutto in medium bowl with chicken, dressing and ⅓ cup of the cheese; toss gently to combine.

4 Trim end from each lettuce; separate leaves (you need 24 small leaves). Place one level tablespoon of the chicken mixture on each leaf; sprinkle with remaining cheese.

preparation time *20 minutes*
cooking time *10 minutes* makes *24*
nutritional count per leaf *2.9g total fat
(0.7g saturated fat); 155kJ (37 cal);
0.7g carbohydrate; 2.1g protein; 0.3g fibre*

You need about a quarter of a large barbecued chicken to get the amount of shredded meat required for this recipe.

oysters with mirin and wasabi

chicken caesar on baby cos leaves

antipasti

1 medium eggplant (300g), sliced thinly
½ cup (125ml) extra virgin olive oil
2 tablespoons fresh basil leaves
400g piece baked ricotta cheese
⅛ teaspoon smoked paprika
¼ teaspoon dried chilli flakes
¼ teaspoon dried oregano leaves
350g cherry tomatoes on the vine
3 chorizo (400g), sliced thickly
¼ cup lightly packed fresh flat-leaf parsley leaves
12 asparagus spears, trimmed
¼ cup (20g) parmesan cheese flakes
10 red radishes (200g), trimmed
1 cup (150g) marinated kalamata olives

1 Brush eggplant slices with 2 tablespoons of the oil; cook on heated oiled barbecue, uncovered, until browned both sides and tender. Drizzle eggplant with another tablespoon of oil; top with basil.

2 Place the ricotta on a shallow oven tray; sprinkle with paprika, chilli and oregano. Place tomatoes on same tray. Drizzle ricotta and tomatoes with 2 tablespoons olive oil; cook in covered barbecue, using indirect heat, following manufacturer's instructions, about 10 minutes or until ricotta is warmed through and tomatoes begin to split.

3 Cook chorizo on heated oiled barbecue, uncovered, until browned both sides. Combine chorizo in medium bowl with parsley.

4 Cook the asparagus in a frying pan of simmering water until just tender; drain. Top asparagus with parmesan; drizzle with remaining olive oil.

5 Serve the eggplant, ricotta, tomatoes, chorizo, asparagus, radishes and olives on a large platter.

preparation time *20 minutes*
cooking time *30 minutes* serves *6*
nutritional count per serving *48.3g total fat
(15.5g saturated fat); 2441kJ (584 cal);
13.7g carbohydrate; 23.4g protein; 3.8g fibre*

To make your own marinated olives, just combine olives with garlic, fresh rosemary and black pepper.

green mango and chilli salad on betel leaves

caprese salad on basil leaves

green mango and chilli salad on betel leaves

3cm piece fresh ginger (15g), grated
2 tablespoons rice vinegar
1 tablespoon peanut oil
2 teaspoons mirin
2 teaspoons soy sauce
½ small green mango (150g), grated coarsely
2 green onions, sliced thinly
1 fresh long red chilli, sliced thinly
½ cup (40g) bean sprouts
½ cup loosely packed fresh coriander leaves
50g snow peas, trimmed, sliced thinly
1 cup (80g) finely shredded wombok
24 large betel leaves

1 Combine ginger, vinegar, oil, mirin and sauce in medium bowl. Add mango, onion, chilli, sprouts, coriander, snow peas and wombok; toss gently to combine.

2 Place one level tablespoon of the mango mixture on each leaf.

preparation time *25 minutes* makes *24*
nutritional count per leaf *0.8g total fat
(0.1g saturated fat); 50kJ (12 cal);
0.8g carbohydrate; 0.3g protein; 0.3g fibre*

Betel leaves are available from Asian food stores. This recipe may be made using crisped iceberg lettuce or spinach instead of the betel leaves, but the flavour will not be the same.
Green mangoes are just immature fruit. They will keep, wrapped in plastic, in the fridge for up to two weeks.

caprese salad on basil leaves

1 small tomato (90g), seeded, chopped finely
40g piece hot pepperoni, chopped finely
50g bocconcini cheese, chopped finely
1 tablespoon olive oil
2 teaspoons balsamic vinegar
24 large fresh basil leaves

1 Place tomato, pepperoni, cheese, oil and vinegar in small bowl; toss gently to combine.

2 Place one rounded teaspoon of the mixture on each basil leaf.

preparation time *20 minutes* makes *24*
nutritional count per leaf *1.7g total fat
(0.5g saturated fat); 79kJ (19 cal);
0.1g carbohydrate; 0.8g protein; 0.1g fibre*

camembert fondue

200g whole camembert cheese
1 tablespoon extra virgin olive oil
1 tablespoon dry white wine
1 clove garlic, crushed
1 teaspoon fresh lemon thyme leaves
1 french stick, sliced thinly

1 Place cheese on large piece of baking paper or foil on an oven tray.

2 Drizzle cheese with oil and wine, then sprinkle with garlic and thyme. Wrap and seal paper or foil to enclose cheese.

3 Cook parcel in covered barbecue, using indirect heat, following manufacturer's instructions, about 20 minutes or until the centre of the cheese is soft.

4 Open paper or foil; dip sliced bread into cheese.

preparation time *10 minutes*
cooking time *20 minutes* serves *6*
nutritional count per serving *13.7g total fat (6.3g saturated fat); 1166kJ (279 cal); 26.6g carbohydrate; 10.7g protein; 1.9g fibre*

Recipe is best made just before serving.

seafood antipasto

12 uncooked large king prawns (840g)
8 sardine fillets (360g)
8 whole cleaned baby octopus (720g)
2 cloves garlic, crushed
2 tablespoons olive oil
440g loaf ciabatta bread, sliced thickly
170g asparagus, halved lengthways
200g grape tomatoes
1 cup (150g) seeded kalamata olives
250g haloumi cheese, sliced lengthways into 8 pieces

garlic chilli dressing
4 cloves garlic, crushed
1 tablespoon finely grated lime rind
¼ cup (60ml) lime juice
2 fresh small red thai chillies, chopped finely

1 Make garlic chilli dressing.

2 Shell and devein prawns, leaving heads and tails intact. Combine prawns in large bowl with sardines, octopus, half the garlic and half the oil. Cover; refrigerate 3 hours or overnight.

3 Combine remaining garlic and oil in small bowl; brush bread slices, both sides, with garlic oil. Toast bread, both sides, on heated oiled barbecue.

4 Cook asparagus, tomatoes, olives and cheese, in batches, on heated oiled barbecue until asparagus is tender.

5 Cook seafood, in batches, on heated oiled barbecue until cooked as desired; drizzle with dressing.

garlic chilli dressing Combine ingredients in screw-top jar; shake well.

preparation time *25 minutes (plus refrigeration time)*
cooking time *20 minutes* serves *4*
nutritional count per serving *51.1g total fat (15.4g saturated fat); 4840kJ (1158 cal); 63.2g carbohydrate; 107.7g protein; 6.2g fibre*

camembert fondue

seafood antipasto

drinks

mixed berry punch

1 black tea bag
1 cup (250ml) boiling water
120g raspberries
150g blueberries
125g strawberries, halved
¼ cup loosely packed fresh mint leaves
3 cups (750ml) chilled sparkling apple cider
2½ cups (625ml) chilled lemonade

1 Place teabag in mug, cover with the boiling water; stand 10 minutes. Discard teabag; cool tea 10 minutes.

2 Using fork, crush raspberries in punch bowl; add blueberries, strawberries, mint and tea. Stir to combine, cover; refrigerate 1 hour.

3 Stir cider and lemonade into punch just before serving; sprinkle with extra mint leaves, if desired.

preparation time *15 minutes (plus refrigeration time)*
makes *2 litres (8 cups)*
nutritional count per cup *0.1g total fat*
(0g saturated fat); 393kJ (94 cal);
21.6g carbohydrate; 0.6g protein; 1.5g fibre

Add fresh fruit and ice cubes to drinks for maximum refreshment on a hot summer day. Prepare and chill the liquid component in advance and chop and add fruit just before guests arrive to keep it fresh and crisp.

pink limeade

1 cup (250ml) lime juice
½ cup (125ml) vodka
2½ cups (625ml) water
1 litre (4 cups) cranberry juice

1 Combine ingredients in large jug. Cover; refrigerate until chilled.

preparation time 5 minutes (plus refrigeration time)
makes 2 litres (8 cups)
nutritional count per cup 0.1g total fat
(0g saturated fat); 447kJ (107 cal);
18g carbohydrate; 0.5g protein; 0.1g fibre

You need approximately eight limes for this recipe.

lemon grass and lime spritzer

⅓ cup (90g) grated palm sugar
½ cup (125ml) water
2 tablespoons coarsely chopped fresh lemon grass
½ cup (125ml) lime juice
3 cups (750ml) chilled sparkling mineral water
1 cup ice cubes

1 Combine sugar and the water in small saucepan; stir, over low heat, until sugar dissolves. Remove from heat; stir in lemon grass. Cover; refrigerate until chilled.

2 Combine strained sugar mixture with juice, mineral water and ice in a large jug.

preparation time 10 minutes (plus refrigeration time)
cooking time 5 minutes makes 1 litre (4 cups)
nutritional count per cup 0.1g total fat
(0g saturated fat); 385kJ (92 cal);
22.2g carbohydrate; 0.3g protein; 0.1g fibre

white sangria

2 large green apples (400g)
½ cup (125ml) lime juice
2 x 750ml bottles medium-dry white wine
½ cup (125ml) white rum
⅓ cup (80ml) apple schnapps
½ cup (80g) pure icing sugar, sifted
3 cups (525g) seedless green grapes, halved
2 cups (300g) blueberries
3 cups (750ml) sparkling mineral water

1 Peel and core apples; slice into thin wedges. Place in medium bowl with juice; stand 5 minutes.

2 Place undrained apples and remaining ingredients into large bowl; stir to combine. Cover; refrigerate 3 hours.

preparation time 10 minutes (plus refrigeration time)
makes 2.5 litres (10 cups)
nutritional count per cup 0.1g total fat
(0g saturated fat); 869kJ (208 cal);
2.1g carbohydrate; 0.8g protein; 1.3g fibre

moroccan mint tea

1 litre (4 cups) hot water
3 black tea bags
1 cup loosely packed fresh mint leaves
2 tablespoons caster sugar
½ cup loosely packed fresh mint leaves, extra
1 cup ice cubes

1 Combine the hot water, tea bags and mint leaves in medium jug; stand 10 minutes.

2 Discard tea bags. Cover tea mixture; refrigerate until cool. Strain tea mixture into medium jug; discard leaves. Stir in sugar, extra mint leaves and ice.

preparation time 10 minutes (plus refrigeration time)
makes 1 litre (4 cups)
nutritional count per cup 0.5g total fat
(0g saturated fat); 209kJ (50 cal);
9.8g carbohydrate; 0.8g protein; 1.4g fibre

pink limeade

white sangria

lemon grass and lime spritzer

moroccan mint tea

party punch

pine-orange and passionfruit frappé

lemon, lime and bitters punch

mango bellini

party punch

2 x 750ml bottles chilled medium-dry white wine
1 tablespoon dark rum
⅓ cup (80ml) peach schnapps
2 tablespoons triple sec
1½ cups (375ml) apple and mandarin juice
3 starfruit (450g), sliced thickly
4 small peaches (460g), sliced thickly

1 Combine wine, rum, schnapps, triple sec and juice in large bowl. Stir in sliced fruit.

2 Refrigerate, covered, for at least an hour before serving.

preparation time *5 minutes (plus refrigeration time)*
makes *2 litres (8 cups)*
nutritional count per cup *1.2g total fat*
(0g saturated fat); 7039kJ (1684 cal);
109.5g carbohydrate; 8.2g protein; 6.3g fibre

We used a traminer riesling for this recipe.

lemon, lime and bitters punch

5 lemon infusion tea bags
1 litre (4 cups) boiling water
1.25 litres (5 cups) lemonade
¼ cup (60ml) lime juice cordial
1 teaspoon aromatic bitters
3 cups ice cubes
2 limes, sliced thinly

1 Combine tea bags and the boiling water in large heatproof jug; stand 5 minutes.

2 Discard tea bags. Cool tea 10 minutes then refrigerate until cold.

3 Just before serving, stir through remaining ingredients.

preparation time *10 mins (plus refrigeration time)*
makes *2.5 litres (10 cups)*
nutritional count per cup *0.1g total fat*
(0g saturated fat); 293kJ (70 cal);
16.5g carbohydrate; 0.2g protein; 0.2g fibre

pine-orange and passionfruit frappé

½ cup (125ml) passionfruit pulp
1 medium pineapple (1.25kg), chopped coarsely
¾ cup (180ml) orange juice
1 teaspoon finely grated orange rind
2 cups crushed ice

1 Strain passionfruit pulp through sieve into small bowl; reserve seeds and liquid separately.

2 Blend or process pineapple, orange juice and reserved passionfruit liquid, in batches, until smooth. Add orange rind and ice; blend until combined. Stir in seeds.

preparation time *15 minutes* makes *1.5 litres (6 cups)*
nutritional count per cup *0.2g total fat*
(0g saturated fat); 284kJ (68 cal);
11.6g carbohydrate; 1.8g protein; 5g fibre

You need six passionfruit for this recipe.

mango bellini

¼ cup (60ml) mango nectar
3 teaspoons mango liqueur
1 teaspoon lime juice
½ cup (125ml) chilled brut Champagne

1 Place nectar, liqueur and juice in a chilled 230ml champagne flute; stir to combine. Top with Champagne.

preparation time *5 minutes* serves *1*
nutritional count per serve *0.1g total fat*
(0g saturated fat); 765kJ (183 cal);
17.2g carbohydrate; 0.6g protein; 0g fibre

virgin sea breeze

2 cups (500ml) chilled cranberry juice
2 cups (500ml) chilled ruby red grapefruit juice
2 tablespoons lime juice

1   Combine ingredients in large jug.

preparation time *5 minutes* makes *1 litre (4 cups)*
nutritional count per cup *0.2g total fat*
(0g saturated fat); 472kJ (113 cal);
26.3g carbohydrate; 1g protein; 0g fibre

tropical punch

1 medium mango (430g), chopped coarsely
200g finely chopped fresh pineapple
250g strawberries, sliced thinly
3 cups (750ml) chilled pineapple juice
1½ cups (375ml) chilled dry ginger ale
½ cup (125ml) orange juice
⅓ cup (80ml) lime juice
⅓ cup (80ml) coconut-flavoured liqueur
⅓ cup (80ml) vodka
2 tablespoons finely shredded fresh mint
crushed ice

1   Combine all ingredients except the ice in large jug.
Serve over ice.

preparation time *15 minutes* makes *2 litres (8 cups)*
nutritional count per cup *0.3g total fat*
(0g saturated fat); 619kJ (148 cal);
23.2g carbohydrate; 1.6g protein; 1.9g fibre

We used Malibu in this recipe, but you can use any
coconut-flavoured liqueur you like.

watermelon refresher

900g coarsely chopped seedless watermelon
½ cup (125ml) chilled orange juice
2 tablespoons lime juice

1   Blend or process ingredients until smooth. Serve
with lime slices.

preparation time *5 minutes* makes *1 litre (4 cups)*
nutritional count per cup *0.5g total fat*
(0g saturated fat); 280kJ (67 cal);
13.8g carbohydrate; 0.9g protein; 1.4g fibre

You need to buy a 1.5kg piece of watermelon to get the
amount of chopped watermelon needed for this recipe.

classic cuba libre

2 tablespoons dark rum
1 tablespoon lime juice
½ cup ice cubes
½ cup (125ml) cola

1   Place rum, juice and ice cubes in a 300ml highball
glass; stir to combine. Top with cola; garnish with lime
wedges, if you like.

preparation time *5 minutes* serves *1*
nutritional count per serve *0g total fat*
(0g saturated fat); 581kJ (139 cal);
13.8g carbohydrate; 0.2g protein; 0g fibre

virgin sea breeze

watermelon refresher

tropical punch

classic cuba libre

starters

prawns with garlic and caper butter, page 46

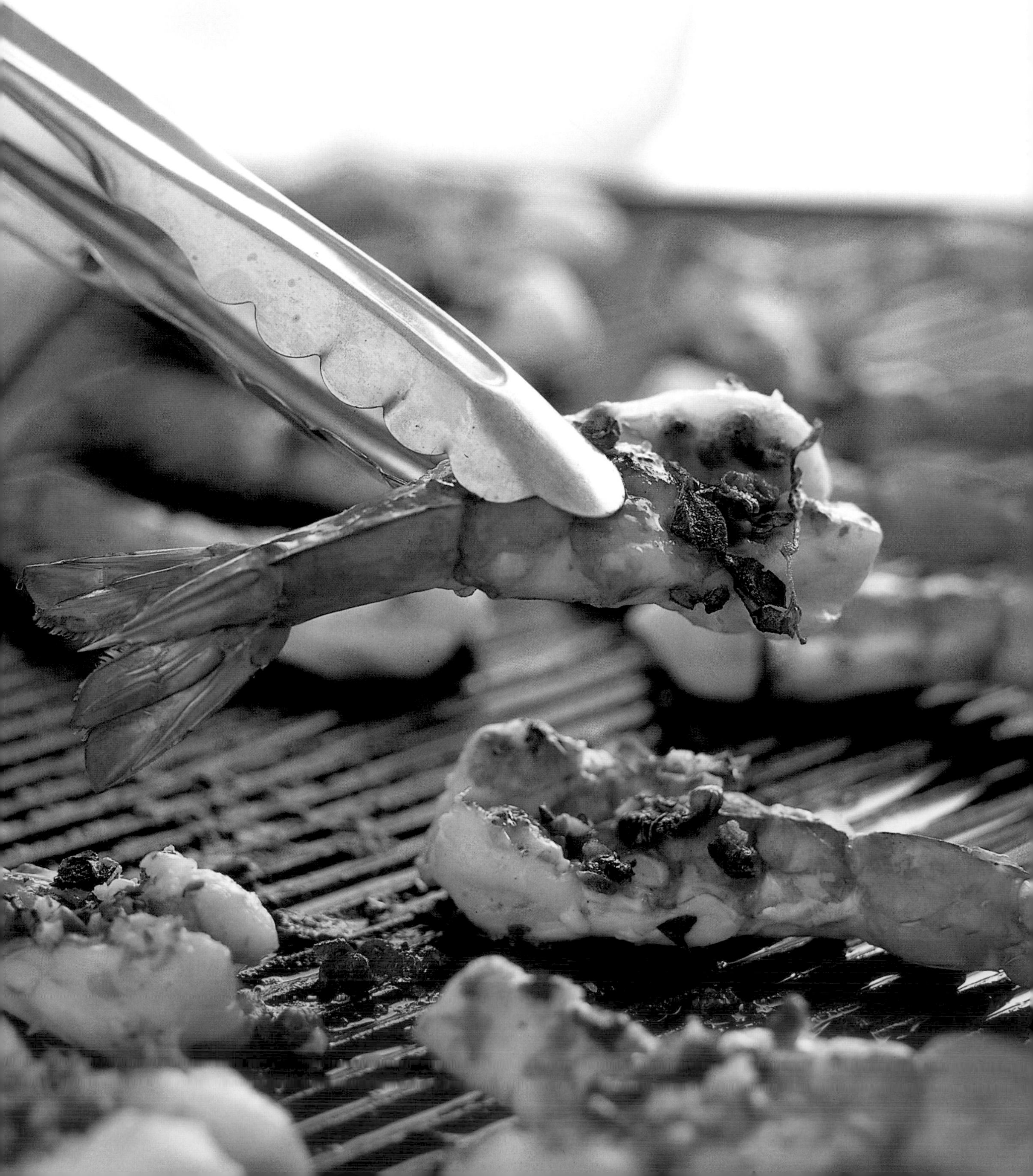

Thread food onto skewers and keep each to a two-bite limit to make it easy to pass around and eat without plates. Soak skewers in water for at least an hour before threading to prevent scorching on the barbecue.

prawns with garlic and caper butter

1kg uncooked large prawns
80g butter
4 cloves garlic, crushed
1 tablespoon rinsed, drained baby capers, chopped coarsely
1 tablespoon finely chopped fresh oregano

1 Peel prawns, leaving tails intact. To butterfly prawns, cut halfway through the back, remove vein then press flat.

2 Melt butter in small saucepan; stir in garlic, capers and oregano. Remove from heat.

3 Cook prawns on heated oiled barbecue until browned on one side; turn, spoon over some of the butter mixture, cook until just cooked through.

4 Serve with remaining butter mixture.

preparation time *20 minutes*
cooking time *10 minutes* serves *4*
nutritional count per serving *17.2g total fat (10.9g saturated fat); 1095kJ (262 cal); 0.8g carbohydrate; 25.9g protein; 0.6g fibre*

tamarind, orange and honey drumettes

2 teaspoons finely grated orange rind
⅓ cup (80ml) orange juice
⅓ cup (120g) honey
⅓ cup (115g) tamarind concentrate
½ cup (125ml) japanese soy sauce
30 chicken drumettes (2kg)
600g baby buk choy, trimmed, quartered
2 medium red capsicums (400g), sliced thickly
230g baby corn
1 tablespoon tamarind concentrate, extra
2 teaspoons sesame oil

1 Combine rind, juice, honey, tamarind and half the sauce in large bowl; add chicken, turn to coat in marinade. Cover; refrigerate 3 hours or overnight.

2 Drain chicken over small bowl; reserve marinade. Cook chicken on heated oiled barbecue, brushing occasionally with reserved marinade, about 30 minutes or until cooked through.

3 Meanwhile, cook buk choy, capsicum and corn on heated oiled barbecue until tender.

4 Place vegetables in medium bowl with combined remaining sauce, extra tamarind and oil; toss to combine. Serve with chicken.

preparation time *15 minutes (plus refrigeration time)*
cooking time *30 minutes* serves *6*
nutritional count per serving *22.3g total fat (6.3g saturated fat); 1994kJ (477 cal); 30.8g carbohydrate; 37g protein; 4.1g fibre*

tamarind, orange and honey drumettes

avocado, olive and bocconcini bruschetta

smoked salmon bruschetta

avocado, olive and bocconcini bruschetta

¼ cup (60ml) olive oil
2 cloves garlic, crushed
4 slices (180g) wholegrain bread
1 medium avocado (250g), chopped coarsely
100g bocconcini cheese, chopped coarsely
¼ cup (30g) seeded black olives, chopped coarsely
1 tablespoon lemon juice
2 medium tomatoes (300g), chopped coarsely

1 Combine half the oil and half the garlic in small bowl. Brush both sides of bread with garlic oil; toast on heated oiled barbecue until browned lightly both sides.

2 Combine avocado, cheese, olives, juice, tomato and remaining oil and garlic in medium bowl.

3 Serve bruschetta topped with avocado mixture.

preparation time *15 minutes*
cooking time *5 minutes* serves *4*
nutritional count per serving *28.8g total fat (6.8g saturated fat); 1693kJ (405 cal); 24.4g carbohydrate; 10.1g protein; 4.5g fibre*

smoked salmon bruschetta

200g crème fraîche
2 tablespoons rinsed, drained baby capers
2 teaspoons finely grated lemon rind
2 teaspoons lemon juice
2 teaspoons finely chopped fresh dill
1 long french bread stick
200g thinly sliced smoked salmon
1 small red onion (100g), sliced thinly
fresh dill sprigs

1 Combine crème fraîche, capers, rind, juice and chopped dill in small bowl.

2 Cut bread into 16 slices; toast on heated oiled barbecue until browned both sides. Spread toast slices with crème fraîche mixture.

3 Divide smoked salmon among toast slices; top each with onion and dill sprigs.

preparation time *15 minutes*
cooking time *5 minutes* serves *8*
nutritional count per serving *12.5g total fat (6.9g saturated fat); 1012kJ (242 cal); 21.6g carbohydrate; 9.9g protein; 1.6g fibre*

raspberry vinaigrette octopus

1kg baby octopus
2 cloves garlic, crushed
⅓ cup (80ml) raspberry vinegar
⅓ cup (80ml) olive oil
¼ cup finely chopped fresh oregano

1 Remove and discard heads and beaks from octopus. Combine octopus with remaining ingredients in large bowl. Cover; refrigerate at least 20 minutes or until required.

2 Drain octopus over small bowl; reserve marinade. Cook octopus on heated oiled barbecue, brushing occasionally with reserved marinade, until just cooked through.

preparation time *15 minutes (plus refrigeration time)* cooking time *10 minutes* serves *4*
nutritional count per serving *20.9g total fat (3.2g saturated fat); 1438kJ (344 cal); 1.6g carbohydrate; 36.9g protein; 0.3g fibre*

lime and coriander octopus

1.5kg baby octopus
2 tablespoons sweet chilli sauce
1 tablespoon kecap manis
¼ cup (60ml) lime juice
2 cloves garlic, crushed
2 tablespoons finely chopped fresh coriander
2 medium limes, sliced thickly

1 Remove and discard heads and beaks from octopus; cut each octopus in half. Combine octopus with sauce, kecap manis, juice, garlic and coriander in large bowl. Cover; refrigerate at least 20 minutes or until required.

2 Drain octopus; discard marinade. Cook octopus and lime slices on heated oiled barbecue until octopus is just cooked through and lime slices are browned both sides.

preparation time *20 minutes (plus refrigeration time)* cooking time *20 minutes* serves *4*
nutritional count per serving *3.7g total fat (0.8g saturated fat); 1053kJ (252 cal); 4.7g carbohydrate; 47g protein; 1.6g fibre*

raspberry vinaigrette octopus

lime and coriander octopus

hoisin pork skewers

chicken yakitori

hoisin pork skewers

750g pork fillet, sliced into thin strips
½ cup (125ml) hoisin sauce
2 tablespoons plum sauce
2 cloves garlic, crushed

1 Combine ingredients in medium bowl. Cover, refrigerate 3 hours or overnight.

2 Thread pork onto 12 skewers. Cook skewers on heated oiled barbecue until browned and cooked through.

preparation time *10 minutes (plus refrigeration time)*
cooking time *10 minutes* makes *12*
nutritional count per skewer *6.3g total fat*
(1.8g saturated fat); 1313kJ (314 cal);
20g carbohydrate; 41.8g protein; 3.8g fibre

You need 12 bamboo skewers for this recipe. Soak them in water for an hour before use to prevent them splintering or scorching during cooking.

chicken yakitori

500g chicken breast fillets
½ cup (125ml) mirin
¼ cup (60ml) kecap manis
1 tablespoon soy sauce
1 teaspoon toasted sesame seeds
1 green onion, sliced thinly

1 Slice chicken into thin diagonal strips; thread strips loosely onto skewers. Place skewers, in single layer, in large shallow dish.

2 Combine mirin, kecap manis and sauce in small jug. Pour half the marinade over skewers; reserve remaining marinade. Cover; refrigerate 3 hours or overnight.

3 Simmer reserved marinade in small saucepan over low heat until reduced by half.

4 Meanwhile, cook drained skewers on heated oiled barbecue until cooked through.

5 Serve skewers drizzled with hot marinade and sprinkled with sesame seeds and onion.

preparation time *20 minutes (plus refrigeration time)*
cooking time *10 minutes* makes *24*
nutritional count per skewer *0.6g total fat*
(0.1g saturated fat); 121kJ (29 cal);
0.3g carbohydrate; 4.9g protein; 0g fibre

You need 24 bamboo skewers for this recipe. Soak them in water for an hour before use to prevent them splintering or scorching during cooking.

prawn sizzlers

2kg uncooked medium prawns
¼ cup (60ml) peanut oil
2 cloves garlic, crushed
2 tablespoons sambal oelek
1½ tablespoons finely chopped fresh thyme

1 Shell and devein prawns, leaving heads and tails intact. Combine prawns with remaining ingredients in large bowl. Cover; refrigerate at least 20 minutes or until required.

2 Cook prawns on heated oiled barbecue until just cooked through.

preparation time *15 minutes (plus refrigeration time)*
cooking time *10 minutes* serves *4*
nutritional count per serving *15.1g total fat (2.7g saturated fat); 1388kJ (332 cal); 2.5g carbohydrate; 46.3g protein; 0.3g fibre*

devilled squid

2 large squid hoods (500g)
¼ cup finely chopped fresh mint

marinade
2 teaspoons finely grated lemon rind
¼ cup (60ml) lemon juice
1 tablespoon peanut oil
2 cloves garlic, crushed
2 teaspoons Tabasco sauce

lime vinaigrette
2 teaspoons white sugar
2 tablespoons lime juice
⅓ cup (80ml) peanut oil
2 cloves garlic, crushed
2 green onions, chopped finely
1 fresh small red thai chilli, sliced thinly

1 Make marinade and lime vinaigrette.

2 Cut squid hoods in half lengthways, then cut lengthways into 1cm strips; thread onto 12 skewers. Combine skewers with marinade in large shallow dish. Cover; refrigerate at least 20 minutes or until required.

3 Drain skewers over small bowl; reserve marinade. Cook skewers on heated oiled barbecue, brushing occasionally with reserved marinade, until just cooked through.

4 Sprinkle skewers with mint; serve with lime vinaigrette.

marinade Combine ingredients in small bowl.

lime vinaigrette Combine ingredients in screw-top jar; shake well.

preparation time *30 minutes (plus refrigeration time)*
cooking time *10 minutes* makes *12*
nutritional count per skewer *24.4g total fat (4.6g saturated fat); 1342kJ (321 cal); 3.4g carbohydrate; 21.4g protein; 0.9g fibre*

You need 12 bamboo skewers for this recipe. Soak them in water for an hour before use to prevent them splintering or scorching during cooking.

prawn sizzlers

devilled squid

goats cheese and garlic bruschetta

lamb and rocket bruschetta

goats cheese and garlic bruschetta

1 loaf ciabatta bread (440g)
¼ cup (60ml) olive oil
2 cloves garlic, crushed
300g goats cheese
¼ small red onion (25g), sliced thinly
2 tablespoons olive oil, extra
50g baby rocket leaves

1 Cut bread into 16 x 1cm-thick slices. Brush one side of bread with combined oil and garlic. Toast bread on heated oiled barbecue until browned lightly both sides.

2 Using a hot, wet knife, slice cheese thinly. Divide cheese evenly among toasted bread. (If cheese is too soft to slice, spread on toast instead.)

3 Top bruschetta with onion, extra oil and rocket leaves.

preparation time *15 minutes*
cooking time *5 minutes* makes *16*
nutritional count per bruschetta *9.4g total fat (2.9g saturated fat); 652kJ (156 cal); 12.7g carbohydrate; 4.9g protein; 0.9g fibre*

lamb and rocket bruschetta

600g lamb backstraps
½ loaf ciabatta bread (220g)
1 clove garlic, crushed
⅓ cup (90g) sun-dried tomato pesto
¼ cup (75g) mayonnaise
2 teaspoons dijon mustard
25g baby rocket leaves

1 Cook lamb on heated oiled barbecue until cooked as desired. Cover lamb; stand 5 minutes then slice thinly.

2 Meanwhile, cut bread into 8 slices; toast on heated oiled barbecue until browned lightly both sides.

3 Rub one side of toast with a little crushed garlic then spread with tomato pesto.

4 Top with combined mayonnaise and mustard. Divide sliced lamb among bruschetta; sprinkle with rocket.

preparation time *15 minutes*
cooking time *15 minutes* makes *8*
nutritional count per serving *11g total fat (2.6g saturated fat); 983kJ (235 cal); 14.4g carbohydrate; 19g protein; 1.2g fibre*

best salads
for barbecues

barbecued fetta on greek salad, page 62

Prepare salads in advance and keep the undressed salad and the dressing separate in the fridge. Combine dressing and salad just before serving to make sure it is fresh and crisp.

barbecued fetta on greek salad

4 x 100g slices fetta cheese
2 teaspoons finely chopped fresh oregano
2 teaspoons finely chopped fresh marjoram
2 cloves garlic, chopped finely
1 tablespoon olive oil
4 thick slices sourdough bread (160g)
100g baby spinach leaves
¾ cup (110g) seeded kalamata olives
⅔ cup (100g) drained semi-dried tomatoes
12 drained marinated quartered
    artichoke hearts (150g)
⅔ cup (110g) rinsed, drained caperberries
2 tablespoons lemon juice

1 Place each slice of cheese on a 20cm-square piece of foil; rub combined herbs, garlic and oil gently into cheese. Wrap foil around cheese to enclose.

2 Place foil parcels on heated barbecue; cook about 5 minutes or until cheese is heated through.

3 Toast bread both sides on heated oiled barbecue until browned lightly.

4 Meanwhile, place spinach, olives, tomato, artichokes, caperberries and juice in large bowl; toss gently.

5 Divide salad among serving plates; top with bread then cheese.

preparation time *15 minutes*
cooking time *5 minutes* serves *4*
nutritional count per serving *31.4g total fat (16.5g saturated fat); 2274kJ (544 cal); 36.7g carbohydrate; 25.8g protein; 7.2g fibre*

bean and tomato salad with mustard hazelnut dressing

200g green beans, trimmed
250g cherry tomatoes, halved

mustard hazelnut dressing
½ cup (70g) roasted hazelnuts, chopped coarsely
2 tablespoons hazelnut oil
2 tablespoons cider vinegar
1 teaspoon wholegrain mustard

1 Boil, steam or microwave beans until tender; drain. Rinse under cold water; drain.

2 Meanwhile, make mustard hazelnut dressing.

3 Combine beans, tomato and dressing in medium bowl; toss gently.

mustard hazelnut dressing Combine ingredients in screw-top jar; shake well.

preparation time *10 minutes*
cooking time *10 minutes* serves *4*
nutritional count per serving *20.2g total fat (1.8g saturated fat); 920kJ (220 cal); 3.6g carbohydrate; 4.2g protein; 4.3g fibre*

bean and tomato salad with mustard hazelnut dressing

crunchy rice and herb salad

vietnamese coleslaw

crunchy rice and herb salad

1 cup (200g) wild rice blend
1 medium red capsicum (200g), sliced thinly
1 small red onion (100g), sliced thinly
⅓ cup (50g) sunflower seed kernels
⅓ cup (65g) pepitas
⅓ cup (50g) roasted unsalted cashews
½ cup coarsely chopped fresh flat-leaf parsley
2 tablespoons coarsely chopped fresh oregano

black pepper dressing
1 teaspoon finely grated lemon rind
¼ cup (60ml) lemon juice
2 tablespoons olive oil
1 teaspoon dijon mustard
1 teaspoon cracked black pepper

1 Cook rice in large saucepan of boiling water, uncovered, until just tender; drain. Rinse under warm water; drain.

2 Meanwhile, make black pepper dressing.

3 Combine rice and dressing in large bowl with remaining ingredients.

black pepper dressing Combine ingredients in screw-top jar; shake well.

preparation time 15 minutes
cooking time 15 minutes serves 4
nutritional count per serving 27.4g total fat
(2.9g saturated fat); 1639kJ (392 cal);
15.7g carbohydrate; 8.3g protein; 6g fibre

vietnamese coleslaw

2 medium carrots (240g)
½ small green papaya (325g)
8 cups (640g) coarsely shredded wombok
½ cup firmly packed fresh mint leaves
½ cup firmly packed fresh coriander leaves
½ cup (75g) roasted crushed unsalted peanuts

lime dressing
¼ cup (60ml) lime juice
1 clove garlic, crushed
1 fresh small red thai chilli, chopped finely
2 tablespoons grated palm sugar
2 tablespoons fish sauce
2 teaspoons peanut oil

1 Make lime dressing.

2 Using vegetable peeler, slice carrots and papaya lengthways into ribbons.

3 Combine carrot and papaya in large bowl with remaining ingredients; add dressing, toss gently.

lime dressing Combine ingredients in screw-top jar; shake well.

preparation time 20 minutes
cooking time 5 minutes serves 8
nutritional count per serving 5.7g total fat
(0.9g saturated fat); 2224kJ (532 cal);
8.6g carbohydrate; 4.1g protein; 3.7g fibre

You need a wombok weighing approximately 1.2kg for this recipe. Salad is best dressed just before serving. Green papayas are just unripe papayas. They are available at Asian food stores; look for one that is hard and slightly shiny, proving it is freshly picked. Papaya will ripen rapidly if not used within a day or two.

potato salad

2kg potatoes
2 tablespoons cider vinegar
4 green onions, sliced thinly
¼ cup finely chopped fresh flat-leaf parsley

mayonnaise
2 egg yolks
2 teaspoons lemon juice
1 teaspoon dijon mustard
1 cup (250ml) vegetable oil
2 tablespoons warm water, approximately

1 Cover whole peeled potatoes with cold water in large saucepan; bring to the boil. Reduce heat; simmer, covered, until tender. Drain; cut potatoes into 3cm pieces. Spread potato on a tray, sprinkle with vinegar; refrigerate until cold.

2 Meanwhile, make mayonnaise.

3 Combine potato, mayonnaise, onion and parsley in large bowl.

mayonnaise Blend or process egg yolks, juice and mustard until smooth. With motor operating, gradually add oil in a thin, steady stream; process until mixture thickens. Add as much of the warm water as required to thin mayonnaise.

preparation time *30 minutes (plus refrigeration time)*
cooking time *15 minutes* serves *8*
nutritional count per serving *30.4g total fat (4.1g saturated fat); 1764kJ (422 cal); 29g carbohydrate; 6.2g protein; 3.7g fibre*

Properly cooked, any waxy, white-fleshed potato, such as desiree, pontiac or bintje, will hold its shape when tossed in a salad.

eggplant, fetta and semi-dried tomato salad

2 medium red capsicums (400g)
8 baby eggplants (480g), halved lengthways
1 medium red onion (170g), cut into wedges
250g fetta cheese, crumbled
350g watercress, trimmed
100g drained semi-dried tomatoes, sliced thinly

creamy horseradish dressing
1 egg
2 tablespoons prepared horseradish
2 teaspoons honey
2 cloves garlic, quartered
⅔ cup (160ml) olive oil

1 Quarter capsicums; discard seeds and membranes. Cook capsicum, eggplant and onion, in batches, on heated oiled barbecue until browned. Cover capsicum in paper or plastic for 5 minutes then peel away skin.

2 Meanwhile, make creamy horseradish dressing.

3 Combine cheese, watercress and tomato in medium bowl; divide among serving plates. Top with capsicum, eggplant and onion; drizzle with dressing.

creamy horseradish dressing Blend or process egg, horseradish, honey and garlic until smooth. With motor operating, add oil in a thin, steady stream until dressing thickens slightly.

preparation time *20 minutes*
cooking time *15 minutes* serves *6*
nutritional count per serving *36.3g total fat (10.2g saturated fat); 1910kJ (457 cal); 14.6g carbohydrate; 15.1g protein; 8.2g fibre*

Make sure you use prepared white horseradish in the dressing and not the blended condiment sold by the name of horseradish cream.

potato salad

eggplant, fetta and semi-dried tomato salad

goats cheese, prosciutto and fig salad

panzanella

goats cheese, prosciutto and fig salad

6 slices prosciutto (90g)
120g baby rocket leaves, trimmed
4 large fresh figs (320g), quartered
150g soft goats cheese, crumbled

honey cider dressing
¼ cup (60ml) cider vinegar
2 tablespoons olive oil
1 tablespoon wholegrain mustard
1 tablespoon honey

1 Make honey cider dressing.

2 Cook prosciutto on heated oiled barbecue until crisp; chop coarsely.

3 Serve rocket topped with fig, cheese and prosciutto; drizzle with dressing.

honey cider dressing Combine ingredients in screw-top jar; shake well.

preparation time *10 minutes*
cooking time *5 minutes* serves *4*
nutritional count per serving *16.9g total fat (5.7g saturated fat); 1062kJ (254 cal); 13.7g carbohydrate; 11.1g protein; 2.6g fibre*

Freeze cheese for 10 minutes to make crumbling easier.

panzanella

1 litre (4 cups) water
250g stale sourdough bread, cut into 2cm slices
2 large tomatoes (440g), chopped coarsely
1 small red onion (100g), sliced thinly
2 lebanese cucumbers (260g), chopped coarsely
1 cup firmly packed fresh basil leaves
2 tablespoons olive oil
2 tablespoons red wine vinegar
1 clove garlic, crushed

1 Place the water in a large shallow bowl; briefly dip bread slices into water. Pat dry with absorbent paper; tear bread into large chunks.

2 Combine bread with remaining ingredients in large bowl; toss gently.

preparation time *20 minutes* serves *4*
nutritional count per serving *11g total fat (1.5g saturated fat); 1104kJ (264 cal); 33.2g carbohydrate; 7.5g protein; 6g fibre*

You need about one-third of a sourdough bread loaf for this recipe.

caesar salad

½ loaf ciabatta bread (220g)
1 clove garlic, crushed
⅓ cup (80ml) olive oil
2 eggs
3 baby cos lettuces, trimmed, leaves separated
1 cup (80g) flaked parmesan cheese

caesar dressing
1 clove garlic, crushed
1 tablespoon dijon mustard
2 tablespoons lemon juice
2 teaspoons worcestershire sauce
2 tablespoons olive oil

1 Cut bread into 2cm cubes; combine garlic and oil in large bowl with bread. Toast bread on oven tray in covered barbecue, using indirect heat, following manufacturer's instructions, about 5 minutes or until croûtons are browned.

2 Meanwhile, make caesar dressing.

3 Bring water to the boil in small saucepan, add eggs; cover pan tightly, remove from heat. Remove eggs from water after 2 minutes. When cool enough to handle, break eggs into large bowl; add lettuce, mixing gently so egg coats lettuce.

4 Add cheese, croûtons and dressing to bowl; toss gently.

caesar dressing Combine ingredients in screw-top jar; shake well.

preparation time *30 minutes*
cooking time *15 minutes* serves *4*
nutritional count per serving *39.1g total fat (9.1g saturated fat); 2366kJ (566 cal); 33.1g carbohydrate; 18.4g protein; 5.6g fibre*

This recipe calls for barely cooked eggs; exercise caution if there is a salmonella problem in your area, particularly children and pregnant women.

pasta salad

250g orecchiette pasta
2 tablespoons drained sun-dried tomatoes, chopped coarsely
1 small red onion (100g), sliced thinly
1 small green capsicum (150g), sliced thinly
½ cup coarsely chopped fresh flat-leaf parsley

sun-dried tomato dressing
1 tablespoon sun-dried tomato pesto
1 tablespoon white wine vinegar
2 tablespoons olive oil

1 Cook pasta in large saucepan of boiling water, uncovered, until just tender; drain. Rinse under cold water; drain.

2 Meanwhile, make sun-dried tomato dressing.

3 Combine pasta with remaining ingredients and dressing in large bowl; toss gently.

sun-dried tomato dressing Combine ingredients in screw-top jar; shake well.

preparation time *15 minutes*
cooking time *10 minutes* serves *4*
nutritional count per serving *12g total fat (1.9g saturated fat); 1405kJ (336 cal); 46g carbohydrate; 8.8g protein; 3.6g fibre*

If you can't find orecchiette, replace it with penne pasta.

caesar salad

pasta salad

tabbouleh

haloumi and pomegranate salad

tabbouleh

¼ cup (40g) burghul
3 medium tomatoes (450g)
3 cups coarsely chopped fresh flat-leaf parsley
3 green onions, chopped finely
¼ cup coarsely chopped fresh mint
¼ cup (60ml) lemon juice
¼ cup (60ml) olive oil

1   Place burghul in medium shallow bowl. Halve tomatoes; scoop pulp from tomato over burghul. Chop tomato flesh finely; spread over burghul along with any juice. Cover; refrigerate 1 hour.

2   Combine burghul mixture in large bowl with remaining ingredients.

preparation time *30 minutes*
(plus refrigeration time) serves *4*
nutritional count per serving *14.1g total fat
(2g saturated fat); 790kJ (189 cal);
9.2g carbohydrate; 3.4g protein; 5.6g fibre*

haloumi and pomegranate salad

1 tablespoon lemon juice
2 tablespoons light olive oil
⅓ cup (80ml) pomegranate pulp
¼ cup firmly packed fresh mint leaves
2 green onions, sliced thinly
125g mizuna
1 medium fennel bulb (300g), trimmed, sliced thinly
360g haloumi cheese, sliced thickly

1   Combine juice, oil, pulp, mint, onion, mizuna and fennel in large bowl.

2   Cook cheese on heated oiled barbecue until browned lightly both sides.

3   Serve salad topped with cheese.

preparation time *15 minutes*
cooking time *5 minutes* serves *4*
nutritional count per serving *24.7g total fat
(11.2g saturated fat); 1400kJ (335 cal);
6.5g carbohydrate; 20.6g protein; 3.5g fibre*

One large pomegranate will hold enough sweet-sour pulp for this recipe.

radicchio and tomato salad

⅓ cup (80ml) olive oil
1 clove garlic, crushed
6 medium egg tomatoes (450g), halved
4 small radicchio (600g), quartered
2 tablespoons balsamic vinegar
100g baby rocket leaves
⅔ cup (50g) shaved pecorino cheese

1 Combine 1 tablespoon of the oil with garlic in small bowl. Place tomato, cut-side up, on oven tray; drizzle with oil mixture. Cook in covered barbecue, using indirect heat, following manufacturer's instructions, about 20 minutes or until softened.

2 Combine radicchio with 2 tablespoons of the remaining oil in large bowl. Cook radicchio on heated oiled barbecue, uncovered, until browned all over; cool 5 minutes.

3 Combine vinegar and remaining oil in screw-top jar; shake well.

4 Arrange tomato, radicchio and rocket on large serving platter; sprinkle with cheese, drizzle with dressing.

preparation time *10 minutes*
cooking time *20 minutes* serves *6*
nutritional count per serving *14.9g total fat
(3.2g saturated fat); 681kJ (163 cal);
2.9g carbohydrate; 4.6g protein; 3g fibre*

avocado caprese salad

4 large vine-ripened tomatoes (480g)
250g cherry bocconcini cheese
1 large avocado (320g), halved
¼ cup loosely packed fresh basil leaves
2 tablespoons olive oil
1 tablespoon balsamic vinegar

1 Slice tomato, cheese and avocado thickly; place slices on serving platter. Top with basil then drizzle with combined oil and vinegar. Sprinkle with freshly ground black pepper, if desired.

preparation time *10 minutes* serves *4*
nutritional count per serving *29g total fat
(10.1g saturated fat); 1342kJ (321 cal);
2.3g carbohydrate; 13.1g protein; 2.3g fibre*

We used vine-ripened truss tomatoes because it takes a simple recipe like this for their brilliant colour, robust flavour and crisp, tangy flesh to stand out at their magnificent best. Use less costly tomatoes to cook with, but always go for these when you're serving them raw.

radicchio and tomato salad

avocado caprese salad

best breads
for barbecues

Fresh bread rolls are a must when sausages are on the menu, but you also can toast bread on a barbecue, or cook pizza, to imbue them with a delicious smoky flavour.

garlic bread

1 loaf turkish bread (430g)
50g butter, melted
2 cloves garlic, crushed
2 tablespoons finely chopped fresh flat-leaf parsley

1   Halve bread horizontally; cut each half into four pieces.

2   Combine butter, garlic and parsley in small bowl; brush over bread pieces.

3   Cook bread on heated oiled barbecue until browned both sides.

preparation time *5 minutes*
cooking time *5 minutes* serves *4*
nutritional count per serving *11.2g total fat (5.9g saturated fat); 1229kJ (294 cal); 38.9g carbohydrate; 7.9g protein; 2.6g fibre*

cheese and olive loaf

1 cup (150g) self-raising flour
⅔ cup (50g) coarsely grated parmesan cheese
2 tablespoons coarsely chopped fresh mint
½ teaspoon ground black pepper
1 cup (120g) seeded black olives, chopped coarsely
75g mortadella, chopped coarsely
4 eggs, beaten lightly
80g butter, melted

1   Preheat oven to 200°C/180°C fan-forced. Lightly grease 8cm x 26cm bar cake pan.

2   Sift flour into medium bowl; stir in cheese, mint, pepper, olives and mortadella. Add egg and butter; stir until well combined.

3   Spread mixture into pan; bake about 35 minutes or until browned lightly. Turn onto wire rack to cool.

preparation time *15 minutes*
cooking time *35 minutes* serves *6*
nutritional count per serving *21.3g total fat (11.2g saturated fat); 1371kJ (328 cal); 22.5g carbohydrate; 12.1g protein; 1.5g fibre*

Recipe can be made a day ahead; keep, covered, in the refrigerator. The loaf is suitable to freeze.

Mortadella is an Italian cured sausage made of pork that is first ground and then mashed into a paste. It is delicately flavoured with spices, including whole or ground black pepper, myrtle berries, nutmeg and coriander. Available from delicatessens.

cheese and olive loaf

barbecued pizza trio

2 teaspoons (7g) dry yeast
½ teaspoon white sugar
¾ cup (180ml) warm water
2 cups (300g) plain flour
1 teaspoon coarse cooking salt
2 tablespoons olive oil
cooking-oil spray
1 tablespoon olive oil, extra

mushroom and olive topping
2 flat mushrooms (160g), sliced thickly
170g asparagus, trimmed
⅓ cup (85g) bottled tomato pasta sauce
2 tablespoons seeded black olives
1 tablespoon rinsed, drained baby capers

tomato and bocconcini topping
3 baby eggplants (180g), sliced thinly lengthways
1 tablespoon basil pesto
2 teaspoons olive oil
2 medium egg tomatoes (150g), sliced thinly
150g bocconcini cheese, sliced thinly
12 fresh basil leaves, torn

potato and pine nut topping
4 baby new potatoes (160g), sliced thinly
2 teaspoons finely chopped fresh rosemary
30g baby spinach leaves
⅓ cup (25g) flaked parmesan cheese
1 tablespoon roasted pine nuts

1 To make pizza dough, combine yeast, sugar and the water in small bowl; cover, stand in warm place about 10 minutes or until frothy.

2 Combine yeast mixture, flour, salt and oil in large bowl; mix to a soft dough.

3 Knead dough on floured surface until elastic. Place dough in oiled large bowl, cover; stand in warm place about 1 hour or until doubled in size.

4 Meanwhile, prepare toppings.

5 Knead dough on floured surface until smooth. Divide dough into thirds. Roll each piece to form 16cm x 40cm pizza base.

6 Layer two pieces of foil, large enough to fit one portion of dough. Spray top of foil with cooking-oil spray. Place one portion of dough on top of foil; repeat so that all three pizza bases sit on double layer of foil.

7 Place pizzas, on foil, on barbecue grill plate; cook, covered, using indirect heat, following manufacturer's instructions, about 4 minutes or until underneath is browned lightly. (If dough puffs up, flatten quickly with an egg slide.)

8 Remove pizza bases from barbecue; close cover. Turn pizza bases over; brush cooked side with extra oil then top with selected toppings, as directed below. Return pizzas to barbecue on foil; cover barbecue, cook 5 minutes or until well browned underneath and crisp.

preparation time *1 hour (plus standing time)*
cooking time *20 minutes* makes *3 thin pizzas*

mushroom and olive Cook mushrooms and asparagus on heated oiled barbecue grill plate until tender. Spread pizza base with pasta sauce. Top with mushrooms, asparagus, olives and capers.

nutritional count per slice *3.4g total fat (0.5g saturated fat); 539kJ (129 cal); 18.5g carbohydrate; 4.6g protein; 2.6g fibre*

tomato and bocconcini Cook eggplant on heated oiled barbecue grill plate until tender. Spread pizza base with combined pesto and oil. Top with tomato, eggplant and cheese. Serve sprinkled with basil.

nutritional count per slice *11.2g total fat (4g saturated fat); 853kJ (204 cal); 16.3g carbohydrate; 8.6g protein; 2.3g fibre*

potato and pine nut Cook potato on heated oiled barbecue grill plate until tender. Sprinkle pizza base with rosemary; top with potato, spinach, cheese and nuts.

nutritional count per slice *6.8g total fat (1.6g saturated fat); 681kJ (163 cal); 18.8g carbohydrate; 5.5g protein; 1.7g fibre*

This dough recipe makes enough for three thin pizza bases, and each of the topping recipes makes enough to cover one pizza base. Each pizza was cut into five slices when serving.

from top: mushroom and olive, tomato and bocconcini, potato and pine nut

spinach and fetta damper

pesto bread

spinach and fetta damper

3½ cups (525g) self-raising flour
1 teaspoon salt
2 teaspoons cracked black pepper
1 tablespoon caster sugar
40g cold butter, chopped coarsely
200g fetta cheese, crumbled
200g baby spinach leaves, chopped finely
½ cup (125ml) buttermilk
1 cup (250ml) water, approximately
1 tablespoon buttermilk, extra
1 tablespoon plain flour, extra

1 Combine flour, salt, pepper and sugar in large
bowl; rub in butter.

2 Stir in cheese, spinach, buttermilk and enough of
the water to make a soft, sticky dough.

3 Turn dough onto floured surface; knead until just
smooth. Divide dough in half; place in oiled disposable
baking dish. Press each dough half into a 10cm round.
Cut a cross in dough, about 1cm deep. Brush with a little
extra buttermilk then sift a little extra flour over dough.

4 Cook damper in covered barbecue, using indirect
heat, following manufacturer's instructions, about
40 minutes or until cooked.

preparation time *20 minutes*
cooking time *40 minutes* serves *6*
nutritional count per serving *14.8g total fat
(9.2g saturated fat); 1986kJ (475 cal);
66.4g carbohydrate; 16.3g protein; 4.4g fibre*

pesto bread

1 loaf ciabatta bread (440g)
¼ cup (60ml) olive oil
¼ cup (65g) basil pesto
¼ cup (65g) char-grilled vegetable pesto

1 Cut bread diagonally into 12 slices. Brush slices
lightly with oil.

2 Cook bread on heated oiled barbecue until
browned lightly both sides.

3 Spread half the slices with basil pesto; spread
remaining slices with char-grilled vegetable pesto.

preparation time *10 minutes*
cooking time *5 minutes* serves *6*
nutritional count per serving *20.7g total fat
(3.6g saturated fat); 1860kJ (445 cal);
51.1g carbohydrate; 11.6g protein; 3.8g fibre*

We used bottled basil pesto and char-grilled
vegetable pesto, available from most supermarkets.

sausages

The secret to juicy, tasty snags is to cook them slowly, without pricking, over a low heat, to keep all the flavoursome juices trapped inside.

herb and garlic sausage coil, page 90

herb and garlic sausage coil

24 thin Italian-style continuous sausages in one length
(1.6kg) (or 2 x 12-sausage lengths)
1 lemon
¼ cup coarsely chopped fresh flat-leaf parsley
2 tablespoons fresh rosemary leaves
2 fresh bay leaves, torn
2 cloves garlic, sliced thinly
½ teaspoon salt
½ teaspoon cracked black pepper
2 teaspoons olive oil

1 Cut the continuous sausage into two 12-sausage
lengths and coil each length into a long tight spiral.
Pierce two large metal skewers at right angles through
each sausage coil to secure it.

2 Using a vegetable peeler or zester, peel rind thinly from
lemon; cut rind into thin strips. Squeeze one tablespoon
of juice from the lemon. Combine rind in small bowl with
juice and remaining ingredients. Sprinkle tops of sausage
coils with half of the rind mixture.

3 Cook sausage coils on heated oiled barbecue until
browned underneath. Turn coils, sprinkle with remaining
rind mixture; cook until sausages are cooked through.

preparation time *15 minutes*
cooking time *10 minutes* serves *8*
nutritional count per serving *51g total fat
(24.6g saturated fat); 2437kJ (583 cal);
4.5g carbohydrate; 23.4g protein; 5.7g fibre*

You will need to order the continuous sausages from
your butcher. You also need 4 large metal skewers for
this recipe, to keep the sausages coiled.

chipolatas with homemade barbecue sauce

1 tablespoon olive oil
1 medium brown onion (150g), chopped finely
1 clove garlic, crushed
4cm piece fresh ginger (20g), grated
1 tablespoon tomato paste
1 tablespoon dijon mustard
¼ cup (50g) brown sugar
2 tablespoons red wine vinegar
⅓ cup (80ml) worcestershire sauce
410g can crushed tomatoes
1kg chipolata sausages

1 Heat oil in medium frying pan; cook onion and garlic
until soft. Add ginger, paste, mustard, sugar, vinegar,
sauce and undrained tomatoes; simmer, uncovered,
about 20 minutes or until thick. Blend or process sauce
until smooth.

2 Meanwhile, cook sausages on heated oiled barbecue
until cooked through. Serve with sauce.

preparation time *10 minutes*
cooking time *30 minutes* serves *4*
nutritional count per serving *68.5g total fat
(31.2g saturated fat); 3449kJ (825 cal);
18.9g carbohydrate; 31.1g protein; 8.9g fibre*

chipolatas with homemade barbecue sauce

sausages with kipflers, onions and mushrooms

sausages with warm pear and witlof salad

sausages with kipflers, onions and mushrooms

750g kipfler potatoes
olive-oil cooking spray
¼ cup coarsely chopped fresh chives
200g swiss brown mushrooms, sliced thickly
8 thick beef sausages (640g)
2 large red onions (600g), sliced thinly
1 tablespoon balsamic vinegar
1 tablespoon brown sugar

1 Boil, steam or microwave unpeeled potatoes until just tender; drain. Place on heated oiled barbecue; spray with oil. Cook potatoes until crisp. Remove from heat; sprinkle with chives.

2 Meanwhile, cook mushrooms and sausages on heated oiled barbecue until mushrooms are browned and sausages are cooked through.

3 Cook onion, stirring, on heated oiled flat plate until soft. Sprinkle with vinegar and sugar; cook, stirring, until onion is caramelised.

4 Divide potatoes, sausages and mushrooms among serving plates; top with onion mixture.

preparation time *10 minutes*
 cooking time *25 minutes* serves *4*
nutritional count per serving *41.9g total fat (19.6g saturated fat); 2746kJ (657 cal); 39g carbohydrate; 26.8g protein; 10.6g fibre*

sausages with warm pear and witlof salad

2 medium red onions (340g), cut into wedges
1 tablespoon caraway seeds
3 medium pears (690g), cut into wedges
¼ cup (60ml) cider vinegar
2 tablespoons olive oil
8 thick pork sausages (960g)
1 cup (140g) roasted pecan nuts
2 witlof (250g), trimmed, leaves separated then halved lengthways

1 Cook onion on heated oiled flat plate until softened. Add caraway seeds and pear; cook about 5 minutes or until pear is browned lightly. Combine pear mixture in medium bowl with vinegar and oil.

2 Meanwhile, cook sausages on heated oiled barbecue until cooked through.

3 Place nuts and witlof in bowl with pear mixture; toss gently to combine. Serve salad with sausages.

preparation time *15 minutes*
cooking time *15 minutes* serves *4*
nutritional count per serving *87.8g total fat (24.5g saturated fat); 4523kJ (1082 cal); 35.2g carbohydrate; 34.4g protein; 12.1g fibre*

merguez with parmesan polenta triangles

1 litre (4 cups) water
1 cup (170g) polenta
20g butter, chopped
1 cup (80g) finely grated parmesan cheese
8 merguez sausages (640g)

summer salad
1 small red onion (100g), chopped finely
4 green onions, sliced thinly
1 lebanese cucumber (130g), seeded, chopped finely
1 trimmed celery stalk (100g), sliced thinly
1 medium yellow capsicum (200g), chopped finely
½ cup loosely packed fresh flat-leaf parsley
½ cup loosely packed fresh mint leaves
2 teaspoons finely grated lemon rind
2 tablespoons lemon juice
2 tablespoons olive oil
1 tablespoon white wine vinegar

1 Oil deep 19cm-square cake pan.

2 Place the water in large saucepan; bring to the boil. Gradually stir polenta into water; simmer, stirring, about 10 minutes or until polenta thickens. Stir in butter and cheese; spread polenta into pan, cool 10 minutes. Cover; refrigerate 3 hours or until firm.

3 Make summer salad.

4 Turn polenta onto board; cut into four squares then into triangles. Cook polenta, both sides, on heated oiled barbecue until browned and hot. Cover to keep warm.

5 Cook sausages on heated oiled barbecue until cooked through. Serve with salad and polenta.

summer salad Combine onions, cucumber, celery, capsicum and herbs in large bowl. Drizzle with combined rind, juice, oil and vinegar; toss gently.

preparation time *25 minutes (plus refrigeration time)*
cooking time *35 minutes* serves *4*
nutritional count per serving *66.8g total fat
(25.7g saturated fat); 3975kJ (951 cal);
38.3g carbohydrate; 44g protein; 4.4g fibre*

sausages with polenta and spicy tomato sauce

beef sausage and lentil salad

sausages with polenta and spicy tomato sauce

1 litre (4 cups) water
1 cup (170g) polenta
1 cup (120g) coarsely grated cheddar cheese
2 teaspoons olive oil
1 medium red onion (170g), sliced thinly
1 clove garlic, crushed
1 fresh small red thai chilli, chopped finely
4 medium tomatoes (600g), chopped coarsely
8 thick pork sausages (960g)

1 Oil deep 19cm-square cake pan.

2 Bring the water to the boil in medium saucepan; gradually stir in polenta. Reduce heat; simmer, stirring, about 10 minutes or until polenta thickens. Stir in cheese; spread polenta into pan, cool 10 minutes. Cover; refrigerate 3 hours or until firm.

3 Meanwhile, to make spicy tomato sauce, heat oil in medium saucepan; cook onion, garlic and chilli, stirring, until onion softens. Add tomato; simmer, covered, until tomato softens.

4 Cut polenta into quarters. Cook polenta and sausages, in batches, on heated oiled barbecue until polenta is browned both sides and sausages are cooked through.

5 Serve sausages on polenta squares, topped with spicy tomato sauce; sprinkle with fresh thyme leaves, if desired.

preparation time *20 minutes (plus refrigeration time)*
cooking time *15 minutes* serves *4*
nutritional count per serving *65.6g total fat (28.3g saturated fat); 3908kJ (935 cal); 42.2g carbohydrate; 42g protein; 6.8g fibre*

beef sausage and lentil salad

2 cups (400g) brown lentils
2 sprigs fresh thyme
20 baby beetroot (500g), trimmed
8 thick beef sausages (1.2kg)
2 teaspoons olive oil
1 large brown onion (200g), chopped finely
2 teaspoons yellow mustard seeds
2 teaspoons ground cumin
1 teaspoon ground coriander
½ cup (125ml) chicken stock
100g baby spinach leaves

thyme dressing
1 teaspoon fresh thyme leaves
1 clove garlic, crushed
½ cup (125ml) red wine vinegar
¼ cup (60ml) olive oil

1 Make thyme dressing.

2 Cook lentils in large saucepan of boiling water with thyme until lentils are tender; drain, discard thyme. Combine lentils in large bowl with half the dressing.

3 Meanwhile, boil, steam or microwave unpeeled beetroot until tender; drain. When cool enough to handle, peel and halve beetroot.

4 Cook sausages on heated oiled barbecue until cooked through. Cover sausages; stand 5 minutes then slice thickly.

5 Heat oil in small saucepan; cook onion, seeds and spices, stirring, until onion softens. Add stock; bring to the boil then remove from heat.

6 Combine onion mixture, spinach, beetroot, sausage and remaining dressing in bowl with lentils.

thyme dressing Combine ingredients in screw-top jar; shake well.

preparation time *30 minutes*
cooking time *40 minutes* serves *4*
nutritional count per serving *94.5g total fat (39.2g saturated fat); 5676kJ (1358 cal); 55.8g carbohydrate; 62.8g protein; 26.4g fibre*

sausages with tomato relish

1 tablespoon olive oil
1 clove garlic, crushed
1 medium brown onion (150g), chopped coarsely
2 large tomatoes (500g), chopped coarsely
1 tablespoon balsamic vinegar
1 teaspoon brown sugar
1 tablespoon torn fresh basil leaves
8 thin pork sausages

1 Heat oil in small saucepan, add garlic and onion; cook, stirring, until browned lightly. Add tomato, vinegar and sugar; simmer, uncovered, stirring occasionally, about 20 minutes or until mixture is reduced by half. Just before serving, stir through basil.

2 Meanwhile, cook sausages on heated oiled barbecue until browned and cooked through.

3 Serve sausages with warm tomato relish. Sprinkle with extra basil leaves, if desired.

preparation time *10 minutes*
cooking time *35 minutes* serves *4*
nutritional count per serving *30.5g total fat (11.1g saturated fat); 1576kJ (377 cal); 9g carbohydrate; 15.8g protein; 3.6g fibre*

sausages with white bean and parsley salad

sausages with pea and bacon mash

sausages with white bean and parsley salad

4 medium egg tomatoes (300g), seeded,
    chopped coarsely
½ small red onion (50g), sliced thinly
1 clove garlic, crushed
⅓ cup (80ml) red wine vinegar
½ cup (125ml) extra virgin olive oil
½ cup coarsely chopped fresh flat-leaf parsley
½ cup loosely packed fresh basil leaves
2 x 400g cans white beans, rinsed, drained
8 italian sausages

1 Combine tomato, onion, garlic, vinegar, oil, herbs
and beans in medium bowl; toss gently.

2 Cook sausages on heated, oiled barbecue until
cooked through. Serve sausages with bean salad.

preparation 10 minutes
cooking 15 minutes serves 4
nutritional count per serving 71.1g total fat
(20.9g saturated fat); 3653kJ (874 cal);
22.5g carbohydrate; 31.9g protein; 12.7g fibre

Canned haricot, cannellini, navy or great northern
beans are all suitable to use in this recipe.

sausages with pea and bacon mash

3 rindless bacon rashers (195g), chopped coarsely
2 medium brown onions (300g), sliced thinly
8 thick beef sausages (640g)
1kg potatoes, quartered
1 cup (250ml) milk, warmed
40g butter
½ cup (60g) frozen peas

1 Cook bacon on heated oiled barbecue until browned
and crisp.

2 Cook onion and sausages on heated oiled barbecue
until onion is soft and sausages are cooked through.

3 Meanwhile, boil, steam or microwave potato until soft;
drain. Mash potato with milk and butter.

4 Boil, steam or microwave peas until just tender; drain.
Stir peas and bacon through mash.

5 Serve mash topped with sausages and onion.

preparation time 10 minutes
cooking time 30 minutes serves 4
nutritional count per serving 55.9g total fat
(28.1g saturated fat); 3457kJ (827 cal);
39.7g carbohydrate; 37.7g protein; 9.4g fibre

seafood

Tender seafood needs a light hand and brief cooking on the barbecue. Remove from the grill when just a little underdone as seafood will continue cooking after being taken off the heat.

lobster with lime and herbs, page 106

lobster with lime and herbs

6 uncooked medium lobster tails (2.5kg)
⅓ cup (80ml) olive oil
2 teaspoons grated lime rind
½ cup (125ml) lime juice
2 cloves garlic, crushed
2 tablespoons coarsely chopped fresh coriander
2 tablespoons coarsely chopped fresh flat-leaf parsley
6 limes, cut into wedges

1   Remove and discard soft shell from underneath lobster tails to expose flesh.

2   Combine oil, rind, juice, garlic, coriander and parsley in large bowl; add lobster. Cover; refrigerate 1 hour.

3   Drain lobster; reserve marinade.

4   Cook lobster on heated oiled barbecue until browned all over and cooked through, brushing lobster occasionally with reserved marinade during cooking. Serve with lime wedges, if you like.

preparation time *20 minutes (plus refrigeration time)*
cooking time *15 minutes* serves *6*
nutritional count per serving *15g total fat
(2.3g saturated fat); 1701kJ (407 cal);
1g carbohydrate; 66g protein; 1.4g fibre*

whiting in vine leaves

16 pickled vine leaves
16 whiting fillets (1.5kg)
¼ cup (60ml) extra virgin olive oil
2 medium eggplants (600g), sliced thickly
8 green banana chillies
8 yellow banana chillies

1   Rinse vine leaves, drain and pat dry. Wrap the centre of each fish fillet in a vine leaf, leaving the ends open. Brush fish parcel, both sides, with some of the olive oil.

2   Brush eggplant with remaining oil. Cook chillies and eggplant on heated oiled barbecue until browned and cooked through. Transfer to a plate; cover to keep warm.

3   Cook fish on heated oiled barbecue until browned both sides and just cooked through.

4   Serve fish with grilled vegetables.

preparation time *15 minutes*
cooking time *20 minutes serves 8*
nutritional count per serving *8.5g total fat
(1.3g saturated fat); 1007kJ (241 cal);
6.3g carbohydrate; 32.4g protein; 4.9g fibre*

Cryovac-packages of vine leaves can be found in Middle-Eastern food shops and some delicatessens; these must be well rinsed and dried before using. Vine leaves are used as wrappers for a large of number of savoury fillings in the cuisines of the Mediterranean.

whiting in vine leaves

bugs with garlic herbed butter

8 uncooked balmain bugs (1.6kg)
4 large flat mushrooms (360g)
100g curly endive, chopped coarsely

herb butter
125g butter, softened
2 teaspoons finely grated lemon rind
2 tablespoons lemon juice
2 tablespoons finely chopped fresh chives
2 tablespoons coarsely chopped fresh flat-leaf parsley
2 tablespoons coarsely chopped fresh tarragon
1 clove garlic, crushed

1 Place bugs upside down on board; cut tail from body, discard body. Using scissors, cut soft shell from underneath tails to expose meat; cut tails in half lengthways. Discard back vein.

2 Make herbed butter.

3 Melt half the herb butter in small saucepan. Brush mushrooms with half the melted butter; cook on heated oiled barbecue until tender.

4 Brush bugs with remaining melted butter mixture; cook on heated oiled barbecue until just cooked through.

5 Serve endive and mushrooms with bug halves; top with remaining herb butter.

herb butter Beat butter, rind and juice in small bowl with electric mixer until light and fluffy. Stir in herbs and garlic.

preparation time *30 minutes*
cooking time *20 minutes* serves *4*
nutritional count per serving *27.1g total fat (17.1g saturated fat); 1584kJ (379 cal); 2.1g carbohydrate; 30.4g protein; 3.2g fibre*

You could also use scampi or large king prawns instead of the balmain bugs.

whole fish and vegetables with chilli basil sauce

4 baby cauliflowers (500g), halved
2 trimmed corn cobs (500g), cut into 2cm rounds
400g baby carrots, trimmed
2 tablespoons olive oil
4 x 240g whole white fish

chilli basil sauce
80g butter
2 fresh small red thai chillies, chopped finely
⅓ cup firmly packed fresh basil leaves, shredded finely
1 tablespoon lemon juice

1 Place vegetables and half the oil in large bowl; toss to combine. Cook vegetables on heated oiled barbecue until browned all over and cooked through.

2 Meanwhile, make chilli basil sauce.

3 Score each fish three times both sides; brush all over with remaining oil. Cook fish on heated oiled barbecue until cooked as desired. Serve fish and vegetables drizzled with sauce.

chilli basil sauce Melt butter in small saucepan; add chilli, basil and juice, stir until combined.

preparation time *20 minutes*
cooking time *30 minutes* serves *4*
nutritional count per serving *32.2g total fat (13.9g saturated fat); 2608kJ (624 cal); 22.7g carbohydrate; 56.4g protein; 9.3g fibre*

We used whole bream in this recipe, but you can use any whole white fish. Fish fillets can be substituted for the whole fish, if you like.

sardines with tomatoes and caper dressing

12 whole sardines (450g)
4 medium egg tomatoes (300g), sliced thickly
1 small red onion (100g), sliced thinly

caper dressing
⅓ cup (80ml) red wine vinegar
¼ cup (60ml) olive oil
1 tablespoon rinsed, drained baby capers
1 clove garlic, crushed
2 tablespoons coarsely chopped fresh flat-leaf parsley

1 To butterfly sardines, remove and discard heads; cut through the underside of fish to the tail. Break backbone at the tail; peel away backbone, trim fish.

2 Cook sardines on heated oiled barbecue until just cooked through.

3 Meanwhile, make caper dressing.

4 Serve sardines on tomato and onion; spoon over caper dressing.

caper dressing Combine ingredients in screw-top jar; shake well.

preparation time *25 minutes*
cooking time *10 minutes* serves *4*
nutritional count per serving *16.3g total fat (2.7g saturated fat); 1091kJ (261 cal); 3.2g carbohydrate; 24.2g protein; 1.5g fibre*

Sardines are available already butterflied from most fishmongers.

whole fish and vegetables with chilli basil sauce

sardines with tomatoes and caper dressing

garfish with sweet cucumber and peanut sauce

18 whole garfish (1.5kg), cleaned
cooking-oil spray

sweet cucumber and peanut sauce
¼ cup (55g) caster sugar
½ cup (125ml) water
¼ cup (60ml) lime juice
1 tablespoon fish sauce
2 fresh long red chillies, sliced thinly
1cm piece fresh ginger (5g), grated
1 lebanese cucumber (130g), seeded, chopped finely
1 green onion, sliced thinly
1 tablespoon coarsely chopped fresh coriander
1 tablespoon coarsely chopped roasted peanuts

1 Make sweet cucumber and peanut sauce.

2 Meanwhile, spray garfish each side with oil. Cook garfish on heated oiled barbecue until browned and cooked through.

3 Serve garfish with sauce and, if desired, thick char-grilled lime slices.

sweet cucumber and peanut sauce Combine sugar and the water in small saucepan; cook, stirring, without boiling, until sugar dissolves. Bring to the boil; simmer, uncovered, until liquid is reduced by half. Remove syrup from heat; stir in juice, sauce, chilli and ginger, cool. Just before serving, stir remaining ingredients into sauce.

preparation time *20 minutes*
cooking time *20 minutes* serves *6*
nutritional count per serving *3.4g total fat (0.7g saturated fat); 782kJ (187 cal); 10.3g carbohydrate; 28.3g protein; 0.6g fibre*

The sweet cucumber and peanut sauce can be made four days ahead; store, covered, in the refrigerator.

2 teaspoons coriander seeds
1 teaspoon cumin seeds
2 cardamom pods, bruised
1 cinnamon stick
1 teaspoon ground turmeric
½ teaspoon chilli powder
2 tablespoons peanut oil
2 cloves garlic, crushed
4 x 265g salmon cutlets
100g baby spinach leaves

lime pickle yogurt
½ cup (140g) yogurt
2 tablespoons lime pickle, chopped finely

kerala-style salmon with lime pickle yogurt

1 Dry-fry coriander, cumin, cardamom and cinnamon in small heated frying pan, stirring, over medium heat until fragrant. Stir in turmeric and chilli powder; remove from heat.

2 Using mortar and pestle, crush spices until ground finely; transfer to large bowl. Stir in oil and garlic, add fish; turn fish to coat in marinade. Cover; refrigerate 30 minutes.

3 Meanwhile, make lime pickle yogurt.

4 Cook fish on heated oiled barbecue until cooked through. Serve fish with spinach and lime pickle yogurt.

lime pickle yogurt Combine ingredients in small bowl.

preparation time *20 minutes (plus refrigeration time)*
cooking time *15 minutes* serves 4
nutritional count per serving *29.3g total fat
(6.7g saturated fat); 2082kJ (498 cal);
3.9g carbohydrate; 54.1g protein; 1.1g fibre*

An Indian speciality, lime pickle is a mixed pickle condiment of limes that adds a hot and spicy taste to meals. Available from Indian food shops.

squid salad with garlic lime dressing

thai fish burger

squid salad with garlic lime dressing

1kg cleaned squid hoods
1 fresh long red chilli, chopped finely
1 tablespoon peanut oil
500g rocket, trimmed
150g snow peas, sliced thinly
227g can rinsed, drained water chestnuts, sliced thinly
½ cup loosely packed fresh coriander leaves
½ cup loosely packed fresh mint leaves

garlic lime dressing
¼ cup (60ml) lime juice
2 cloves garlic, crushed
2 tablespoons fish sauce
2 tablespoons grated palm sugar
2 green onions, sliced thinly
1 fresh long red chilli, chopped finely
1 tablespoon peanut oil

1 Make garlic lime dressing.

2 Cut squid down centre to open out; score inside in diagonal pattern then cut into thick strips.

3 Combine squid, chilli and oil in medium bowl. Combine remaining ingredients in large bowl.

4 Cook squid on heated oiled barbecue until just cooked through. Combine squid in large bowl with salad and dressing.

garlic lime dressing Combine ingredients in screw-top jar; shake well.

preparation time *25 minutes*
cooking time *10 minutes* serves *4*
nutritional count per serving *11.8g total fat*
(2.1g saturated fat); 1133kJ (271 cal);
15.3g carbohydrate; 23.9g protein; 4.6g fibre

thai fish burger

500g white fish fillets, chopped coarsely
1 tablespoon fish sauce
1 tablespoon kecap manis
1 clove garlic, quartered
1 fresh small red thai chilli, chopped coarsely
50g green beans, trimmed, chopped coarsely
¼ cup (20g) fried shallots
¼ cup coarsely chopped fresh coriander
60g baby spinach leaves
1 lebanese cucumber (130g), seeded, sliced thinly
1 tablespoon lime juice
2 teaspoons brown sugar
2 teaspoons fish sauce, extra
4 hamburger buns (360g)
⅓ cup (80ml) sweet chilli sauce

1 Blend or process fish, fish sauce, kecap manis, garlic and chilli until smooth. Combine fish mixture in large bowl with beans, shallots and coriander; shape into four patties.

2 Cook patties on heated oiled barbecue until just cooked through.

3 Meanwhile, combine spinach, cucumber, juice, sugar and extra fish sauce in medium bowl.

4 Split buns in half; toast cut-sides. Sandwich salad, patties and sweet chilli sauce between bun halves.

preparation time *20 minutes*
cooking time *15 minutes* serves *4*
nutritional count per serving *5.3g total fat*
(0.7g saturated fat); 1722kJ (412 cal);
55.2g carbohydrate; 32g protein; 5.7g fibre

We used blue-eye here, but any firm white fish fillets, such as bream, swordfish, ling or whiting, can be used. Check for any small pieces of bone in the fillets and use tweezers to remove them.

Fried shallots are a staple in the Thai kitchen, used variously as an ingredient when stir-frying, sprinkled over just-cooked dishes or presented as a condiment at the table. Here we've used them to add crunch to the burger mixture. They can be purchased already made from Asian grocery stores or you can fry your own; they'll keep for months if stored tightly sealed.

Skordalia, the classic Greek accompaniment for grilled meats or seafood, is made from mashed potato and/or white bread pureed with garlic, olive oil and lemon juice or vinegar.

fish skewers with potato smash and skordalia

800g white fish fillets, cut into 2cm pieces
¼ cup (60ml) olive oil
2 tablespoons finely chopped fresh flat-leaf parsley
2 tablespoons finely chopped fresh lemon thyme
1kg baby new potatoes, unpeeled
½ cup (120g) sour cream
40g butter, softened

skordalia
1 small potato (120g)
1 slice white bread
2 cloves garlic, crushed
1 tablespoon cider vinegar
¼ cup (60ml) water
2 tablespoons olive oil

1 Thread fish onto eight skewers; place in medium shallow dish. Brush with combined oil and herbs. Cover; refrigerate 20 minutes.

2 Meanwhile, make skordalia.

3 Boil, steam or microwave potatoes until tender; drain. Mash half the potatoes in medium bowl with sour cream and butter until smooth. Using fork, crush remaining potatoes until skins burst; fold into mash mixture. Cover potato smash to keep warm.

4 Cook skewers on heated oiled barbecue until cooked through. Serve smash with fish skewers and skordalia.

skordalia Boil, steam or microwave peeled potato until tender; drain. Mash potato in medium bowl until smooth. Discard crusts from bread. Soak bread in small bowl of cold water; drain. Squeeze out excess water. Blend or process bread with remaining ingredients until smooth. Stir bread mixture into mashed potato.

preparation time *20 minutes (plus refrigeration time)* cooking time *30 minutes* serves *4*
nutritional count per serving *44.7g total fat (16.7g saturated fat); 3114kJ (745 cal); 39.8g carbohydrate; 42.9g protein; 5.3g fibre*

We used blue-eye fillets in this recipe, but you can use any firm white fish fillets you like: bream, flathead, swordfish, ling, whiting, jewfish, snapper or sea perch are all good choices. Check for any small pieces of bone in the fillets and use tweezers to remove them.

You need to soak eight bamboo skewers in cold water for an hour before using to prevent them from splintering and scorching during cooking.

chilli prawns with fresh mango salad

1kg uncooked large king prawns
½ teaspoon ground turmeric
1 teaspoon chilli powder
2 teaspoons sweet paprika
2 cloves garlic, crushed

fresh mango salad
2 large mangoes (1.2kg), chopped coarsely
1 small red onion (100g), sliced thinly
1 fresh long red chilli, sliced thinly
1½ cups (120g) bean sprouts
½ cup coarsely chopped fresh coriander
2 teaspoons fish sauce
2 teaspoons grated palm sugar
2 tablespoons lime juice
1 tablespoon peanut oil

1 Make fresh mango salad.

2 Shell and devein prawns, leaving tails intact. Combine turmeric, chilli, paprika and garlic in large bowl; add prawns, toss to coat in chilli mixture.

3 Cook prawns on heated oiled barbecue until browned lightly. Serve prawns with salad.

fresh mango salad Combine ingredients in medium bowl; toss gently.

preparation time *25 minutes*
cooking time *10 minutes* serves 4
nutritional count per serving *5.9g total fat
(1g saturated fat); 1229kJ (294 cal);
30.3g carbohydrate; 29.5g protein; 5.1g fibre*

fish fillets with fennel and onion salad

1 medium red onion (170g), sliced thinly
4 green onions, sliced thinly
1 large fennel bulb (550g), trimmed, sliced thinly
2 trimmed celery stalks (200g), sliced thinly
½ cup coarsely chopped fresh flat-leaf parsley
⅓ cup (80ml) orange juice
¼ cup (60ml) olive oil
2 cloves garlic, crushed
2 teaspoons sambal oelek
4 x 275g white fish fillets, skin on

1 Combine onions, fennel, celery and parsley in medium bowl.

2 Combine juice, oil, garlic and sambal in screw-top jar; shake well.

3 Cook fish on heated oiled barbecue until browned both sides and cooked as desired.

4 Pour half the dressing over salad in bowl; toss gently to combine. Serve salad topped with fish; drizzle with remaining dressing.

preparation time *15 minutes*
cooking time *10 minutes* serves *4*
nutritional count per serving *20g total fat
(3.9g saturated fat); 1898kJ (454 cal);
8g carbohydrate; 58.3g protein; 4.5g fibre*

We used snapper fillets in this recipe, but you can use any firm white fish fillets you like: bream, flathead, swordfish, ling, whiting, jewfish, blue-eye or sea perch are all good choices. Check for any small pieces of bone in the fillets and use tweezers to remove them.

mussels with beer

1kg large black mussels
1 tablespoon olive oil
2 cloves garlic, crushed
1 large red onion (300g), sliced thinly
2 fresh long red chillies, sliced thinly
1½ cups (375ml) beer
2 tablespoons sweet chilli sauce
1 cup coarsely chopped fresh flat-leaf parsley

garlic bread
1 loaf turkish bread (430g)
50g butter, melted
2 cloves garlic, crushed
2 tablespoons finely chopped fresh flat-leaf parsley

1 Scrub mussels; remove beards.

2 Make garlic bread.

3 Heat oil on heated barbecue flat plate; cook garlic, onion and chilli, stirring, until onion softens. Add mussels and combined beer and sauce; cover with wok lid (or cook in covered barbecue). Cook about 5 minutes or until mussels open (discard any that do not). Remove from heat; stir in parsley.

4 Serve mussels with garlic bread.

garlic bread Halve bread horizontally; cut each half into four pieces, brush with combined butter, garlic and parsley. Cook bread on heated oiled barbecue until browned both sides; keep warm.

preparation time *20 minutes*
cooking time *15 minutes* serves *4*
nutritional count per serving *19.7g total fat
(8.3g saturated fat); 2174kJ (520 cal);
58.3g carbohydrate; 17.6g protein; 5.6g fibre*

Any large, domed, handled, heat-resistant lid you have will do to cover the mussels, so long as it has room for the mussels to steam. Be careful when lifting off the lid, to avoid steam scalds.

fish fillets with fennel and onion salad

mussels with beer

cajun fish

salmon green curry

cajun fish

2 teaspoons sweet paprika
2 teaspoons ground cumin
2 teaspoons ground coriander
2 teaspoons mustard powder
2 teaspoons fennel seeds
¼ teaspoon cayenne pepper
4 x 200g white fish fillets
2 teaspoons olive oil
1 small red onion (100g), sliced thinly
1 large tomato (220g), chopped finely
420g can kidney beans, rinsed, drained

1 Combine paprika, cumin, coriander, mustard, fennel and cayenne in small bowl. Rub mixture onto fish.

2 Cook fish on heated oiled barbecue until just cooked through.

3 Meanwhile, heat oil in small frying pan, add onion and tomato; cook, stirring, until onion is soft. Add beans; stir until hot. Serve bean mixture topped with fish.

preparation time *15 minutes*
cooking time *10 minutes* serves *4*
nutritional count per serving *7.4g total fat*
(2g saturated fat); 1325kJ (317 cal);
12.5g carbohydrate; 46.7g protein; 5.6g fibre

We used kingfish fillets in this recipe, but you can use any firm white fish fillets you like: bream, flathead, swordfish, ling, whiting, jewfish, snapper or sea perch are all good choices. Check for any small pieces of bone in the fillets and use tweezers to remove them.

salmon green curry

2 tablespoons green curry paste
4 x 200g salmon fillets
⅓ cup coarsely chopped roasted unsalted cashews
⅓ cup coarsely chopped fresh coriander
1 tablespoon vegetable oil
1 teaspoon finely grated lime rind
1 tablespoon lime juice

1 Rub curry paste onto fish. Cook fish on heated oiled barbecue until cooked as desired.

2 Meanwhile, combine nuts, coriander, oil, rind and juice in small bowl. Serve fish topped with herb and nut mixture.

preparation time *15 minutes*
cooking time *5 minutes* serves *4*
nutritional count per serving *28.1g total fat*
(5.1g saturated fat); 1814kJ (434 cal);
3g carbohydrate; 41.7g protein; 2g fibre

fish cutlets with mango salsa

4 x 200g white fish cutlets
2 tablespoons lime juice
1 tablespoon fish sauce
1 tablespoon peanut oil
1 tablespoon grated palm sugar
1 teaspoon sambal oelek
2 kaffir lime leaves, shredded finely

mango salsa
2 large mangoes (1.2kg), chopped coarsely
2 lebanese cucumbers (260g), seeded,
   chopped coarsely
1 fresh long red chilli, sliced thinly
½ cup coarsely chopped fresh mint

1 Make mango salsa.

2 Cook fish on heated oiled barbecue, uncovered, until browned both sides and cooked as desired.

3 Combine remaining ingredients in screw-top jar; shake well. Divide salsa and fish among serving plates; drizzle with dressing.

mango salsa Combine ingredients in medium bowl; toss gently.

preparation time *25 minutes*
cooking time *15 minutes* serves *4*
nutritional count per serving *6.5g total fat*
(1g saturated fat); 1463kJ (350 cal);
31.8g carbohydrate; 38.1g protein; 4.3g fibre

We used blue-eye cutlets in this recipe, but you can use any firm white fish cutlets you like. Check for any small pieces of bone in the fillets and use tweezers to remove them.

spicy fish kebabs

1kg firm white fish fillets
1 tablespoon finely chopped fresh mint
1 tablespoon finely chopped fresh coriander
1 tablespoon finely chopped fresh flat-leaf parsley
2 fresh small red thai chillies, chopped finely
2 tablespoons lemon juice
1 tablespoon peanut oil
4 x 10cm sticks fresh lemon grass (80g)

1 Cut fish into 2cm cubes. Combine fish with herbs, chilli, juice and oil in medium bowl.

2 Cut lemon grass stems in half crossways; thread fish onto lemon grass skewers.

3 Cook fish on heated oiled barbecue until cooked through. Serve with lime wedges, if desired.

preparation time *15 minutes*
cooking time *10 minutes* serves *4*
nutritional count per serving *6.3g total fat*
(1.1g saturated fat); 986kJ (236 cal);
0.4g carbohydrate; 43.9g protein; 0.2g fibre

Pierce the fish with a bamboo or metal skewer first, this will make it easier to thread through the lemon grass skewers. You can use bamboo skewers if you prefer; soak them in water for at least an hour before using to prevent them from scorching and splintering during cooking.

fish cutlets with mango salsa

spicy fish kebabs

salt and pepper salmon with wasabi mayo

fish steaks with mediterranean vegetables

salt and pepper salmon with wasabi mayo

2 teaspoons sea salt
2 teaspoons sichuan pepper
1½ tablespoons vegetable oil
4 x 200g salmon fillets, skin on
½ cup (150g) mayonnaise
2 teaspoons wasabi paste
1 teaspoon finely chopped fresh coriander
1 teaspoon lime juice

1 Using mortar and pestle or pepper grinder, grind salt and pepper until fine. Combine pepper mixture, oil and fish in large bowl, cover; stand 5 minutes.

2 Meanwhile, combine mayonnaise, wasabi, coriander and juice in small bowl.

3 Cook fish on heated oiled barbecue until cooked as desired. Serve fish with wasabi mayonnaise, and watercress, if desired.

preparation time *10 minutes*
cooking time *15 minutes* serves *4*
nutritional count per serving *40.1g total fat (6.3g saturated fat); 2278kJ (545 cal); 7.5g carbohydrate; 39.4 protein; 0.2g fibre*

fish steaks with mediterranean vegetables

1 medium red capsicum (200g), sliced thickly
1 medium yellow capsicum (200g), sliced thickly
1 medium eggplant (300g), sliced thickly
2 large zucchini (300g), sliced thickly
½ cup (125ml) olive oil
250g cherry tomatoes
¼ cup (60ml) balsamic vinegar
1 clove garlic, crushed
2 teaspoons white sugar
4 x 220g white fish steaks
¼ cup coarsely chopped fresh basil

1 Combine capsicums, eggplant and zucchini with 2 tablespoons of the oil in large disposable baking dish. Cook in covered barbecue, using indirect heat, following manufacturer's instructions, about 15 minutes. Add tomatoes; cook about 5 minutes or until vegetables are just tender; cover to keep warm.

2 Combine remaining oil, vinegar, garlic and sugar in screw-top jar; shake well. Brush a third of the dressing over fish; cook on heated oiled barbecue, uncovered, until browned both sides and cooked as desired.

3 Combine vegetables in large bowl with basil and remaining dressing; toss gently to combine. Divide vegetables among serving plates; top with fish.

preparation time *20 minutes*
cooking time *25 minutes* serves *4*
nutritional count per serving *33.9g total fat (5.6g saturated fat); 2270kJ (543 cal); 9.3g carbohydrate; 48.2g protein; 4.8g fibre*

We used swordfish steaks in this recipe, but any firm white fish steaks can be used.

calamari with fetta and chilli stuffing

8 whole calamari with tentacles (600g)
400g firm fetta cheese
1 teaspoon dried chilli flakes
2 tablespoons finely chopped fresh oregano
2 tablespoons olive oil
2 teaspoons grated lemon rind
2 tablespoons lemon juice
2 tablespoons finely chopped fresh oregano, extra
1 clove garlic, crushed
¼ cup (60ml) olive oil
1 medium lemon, cut in wedges

1   To clean the calamari, pull gently on the tentacles to remove. Cut tentacles off below the eyes; discard eyes, the small black beak in the centre of the tentacles and intestines. Remove the clear quill from inside the body. Dip fingers into salt, then remove the side flaps and dark membrane (the salt gives a better grip). Rinse well and pat dry.

2   Mash fetta, chilli, oregano and oil in small bowl. Fill calamari tubes with fetta mixture. Use toothpicks to secure opening. Place calamari and tentacles in shallow dish.

3   Combine remaining ingredients, except lemon wedges, in a jug; pour over calamari. Cover; refrigerate 3 hours, turning occasionally.

4   Cook calamari and tentacles on heated oiled barbecue until just cooked through. Serve calamari with lemon.

preparation time *40 minutes (plus refrigeration time)*
cooking time *10 minutes* serves *4*
nutritional count per serving *46.9g total fat
(18.8g saturated fat); 2232kJ (534 cal);
0.7g carbohydrate; 28.7g protein; 0.2g fibre*

Try to find small calamari as they will be more tender. Cuttlefish are also suitable for this recipe.

fish fillets with tomato, caper and walnut dressing

kaffir lime and lemon grass trout

fish fillets with tomato, caper and walnut dressing

4 x 185g white fish fillets

tomato, caper and walnut dressing
250g cherry tomatoes
60g butter
1 tablespoon finely grated lemon rind
2 teaspoons lemon juice
1 teaspoon rinsed, drained capers, chopped finely
¼ cup (30g) finely chopped walnuts
½ cup coarsely chopped fresh flat-leaf parsley

1 Make tomato, caper and walnut dressing.

2 Cook fish on heated oiled barbecue until just cooked through. Serve fish with dressing.

tomato, caper and walnut dressing Cook tomatoes on heated oiled barbecue until tender. Melt butter in small saucepan, add tomatoes and remaining ingredients; stir until hot.

preparation time *15 minutes*
cooking time *20 minutes* serves *4*
nutritional count per serving *19.8g total fat*
(9.2g saturated fat); 1471kJ (352 cal);
2g carbohydrate; 40.1g protein; 1.9g fibre

We used barramundi fillets in this recipe, but you can use any firm white fish fillets you like: bream, flathead, swordfish, ling, whiting, jewfish, snapper, blue-eye or sea perch are all good choices. Check for any small pieces of bone in the fillets and use tweezers to remove them.

kaffir lime and lemon grass trout

10cm stick fresh lemon grass (20g), chopped coarsely
4cm piece fresh ginger (20g), sliced thickly
2 cloves garlic, quartered
2 tablespoons peanut oil
1 tablespoon sweet chilli sauce
1 tablespoon lime juice
2 green onions, chopped finely
1 whole ocean trout (2.5kg)
1 lime, peeled, sliced thinly
10cm stick fresh lemon grass (20g), sliced diagonally
1 kaffir lime leaf, shredded thinly
⅓ cup loosely packed fresh coriander leaves
1 lime, cut into wedges

1 Blend or process chopped lemon grass, ginger, garlic, oil, sauce and juice until smooth. Stir in onion.

2 Place a long piece of baking paper on bench; place fish on paper. Fill cavity with lemon grass mixture.

3 Score fish three times both sides through thickest part of flesh. Seal cuts with lime slices; sprinkle fish with sliced lemon grass and lime leaf. Fold paper over fish to completely enclose, then wrap fish tightly in foil.

4 Cook fish on heated oiled barbecue 25 minutes; turn, cook about 20 minutes or until cooked through.

5 Serve fish sprinkled with coriander; serve with wedges.

preparation time *20 minutes*
cooking time *45 minutes* serves *6*
nutritional count per serving *14.3g total fat*
(3g saturated fat); 1262kJ (302 cal);
1.2g carbohydrate; 41.4g protein; 0.7g fibre

poultry

When cooking poultry directly on the barbecue grill, it only needs moderately-hot heat; place food on the edges of the barbecue where the heat is less fierce. Cuts on the bone tend to be juicier, so drumsticks, legs and wings are ideal barbecue choices.

portuguese-style chicken

3 fresh small red thai chillies, chopped finely
2 teaspoons dried chilli flakes
3 cloves garlic, crushed
¼ cup (60ml) cider vinegar
2 teaspoons finely grated lemon rind
⅔ cup (160ml) lemon juice
2 teaspoons smoked paprika
½ cup finely chopped fresh flat-leaf parsley
2 teaspoons coarse cooking salt
¼ teaspoon cracked black pepper
2 tablespoons olive oil
4 chicken marylands (1.5kg)
80g mesclun

1 Combine chillies, garlic, vinegar, rind, juice, paprika, parsley, salt, pepper and oil in large bowl; add chicken, turn to coat in marinade. Cover; refrigerate 3 hours or overnight.

2 Cook chicken in covered barbecue, using indirect heat, following manufacturer's instructions, about 40 minutes or until cooked through.

3 Serve chicken with mesclun and lemon wedges.

preparation time *15 minutes (plus refrigeration time)*
cooking time *40 minutes serves 4*
nutritional count per serving *41.8g total fat
(11.7g saturated fat); 2337kJ (559 cal);
1.5g carbohydrate; 43g protein; 1.1g fibre*

Sometimes sold as spring salad mix, mesclun is a commercial assortment of young green leaves, and will usually include some or all of the following: rocket, mizuna, baby spinach, curly endive, oak leaf, radicchio and mignonette.

salt and pepper chicken skewers on baby buk choy

8 chicken thigh fillets (880g), chopped coarsely
½ teaspoon five-spice powder
1 teaspoon sichuan peppercorns, crushed
2 teaspoons sea salt
1 teaspoon sesame oil
600g baby buk choy, quartered
1 tablespoon oyster sauce
1 teaspoon soy sauce
1 tablespoon coarsely chopped fresh coriander

1 Thread chicken onto 12 skewers. Combine five-spice, peppercorns and salt in small bowl; sprinkle mixture over chicken, then press in firmly.

2 Cook chicken on heated oiled barbecue until browned and cooked through.

3 Meanwhile, heat oil in wok; stir-fry buk choy with combined sauces until just wilted.

4 Divide buk choy among serving plates; top with chicken skewers. Serve sprinkled with coriander.

preparation time *15 minutes*
cooking time *20 minutes serves 4*
nutritional count per serving *17.4g total fat
(5g saturated fat); 1438kJ (344 cal);
3.2g carbohydrate; 42.9g protein; 2.1g fibre*

You need 12 bamboo skewers for this recipe. Soak them in cold water for at least an hour before using to prevent them splintering and scorching during cooking.

salt and pepper chicken skewers on baby buk choy

lemon thyme and chilli chicken

4 x 500g small chickens
½ cup (125ml) water
1 tablespoon fresh lemon thyme leaves

lemon thyme and chilli marinade
2 fresh long red chillies, chopped finely
2 cloves garlic, crushed
1 tablespoon fresh lemon thyme leaves
2 teaspoons finely grated lemon rind
¼ cup (60ml) lemon juice
2 tablespoons olive oil
2 tablespoons balsamic vinegar
2 tablespoons honey

1 Make lemon thyme and chilli marinade.

2 Discard necks from chickens. Using scissors, cut along each side of backbones; discard backbones. Turn chickens skin-side up; press down on breastbone to flatten. Cut each chicken into quarters.

3 Combine three-quarters of the marinade with chicken in large shallow dish, turning to coat all over in marinade. Cover; refrigerate 3 hours or overnight. Refrigerate remaining marinade, covered, until required.

4 Divide the water between two large disposable baking dishes; place chicken, in single layer, on wire racks over baking dishes. Cook chicken in covered barbecue, using indirect heat, following manufacturer's instructions, about 40 minutes or until cooked through.

5 Meanwhile, reheat reserved marinade in small saucepan. Place chicken on serving platter; drizzle with warm marinade and sprinkle with thyme leaves.

lemon thyme and chilli marinade Combine ingredients in screw-top jar; shake well.

preparation time *30 minutes (plus refrigeration time)*
cooking time *40 minutes* serves *10*
nutritional count per serving *23.4g total fat (6.7g saturated fat); 1363kJ (326 cal); 4.7g carbohydrate; 24.6g protein; 0.1g fibre*

sesame wasabi chicken with daikon salad

1 tablespoon japanese soy sauce
1 tablespoon sesame oil
2 tablespoons wasabi paste
8 chicken drumsticks (1.5kg)

daikon salad
2 medium carrots (240g)
1 small daikon (400g)
6 green onions, sliced thinly
1 tablespoon mirin
1 tablespoon lime juice
2 teaspoons sesame oil
2 teaspoons japanese soy sauce
2 tablespoons toasted sesame seeds

1 Combine sauce, oil and paste in large bowl; add chicken, turn to coat in mixture.

2 Cook chicken on heated oiled barbecue, turning and brushing occasionally with marinade, about 40 minutes or until cooked through.

3 Meanwhile, make daikon salad. Serve chicken with salad.

daikon salad Using vegetable peeler, slice carrots and daikon into ribbons. Place in large bowl with remaining ingredients; toss to combine.

*preparation time 20 minutes
cooking time 40 minutes serves 4
nutritional count per serving 31.3g total fat
(7.7g saturated fat); 1948kJ (466 cal);
7.2g carbohydrate; 36.5g protein; 4.1g fibre*

fontina, pancetta and sage chicken

4 x 200g chicken breast fillets
4 thin slices fontina cheese (100g)
4 slices pancetta (60g)
2 tablespoons coarsely chopped fresh sage
2 tablespoons olive oil
2 cloves garlic, crushed
16 whole sage leaves

1 Slit a pocket in one side of each chicken fillet but do not cut all the way through. Divide cheese, pancetta and chopped sage among pockets; secure with toothpicks. Brush chicken with combined oil and garlic.

2 Cook chicken on heated oiled barbecue until browned both sides and cooked through. Remove toothpicks before serving.

3 Cook whole sage leaves on heated oiled barbecue until golden brown. Serve chicken topped with sage leaves.

*preparation time 15 minutes
cooking time 20 minutes serves 4
nutritional count per serving 23.3g total fat
(8g saturated fat); 1806kJ (432 cal);
0.3g carbohydrate; 55.3g protein; 0.3g fibre*

sesame wasabi chicken with daikon salad

fontina, pancetta and sage chicken

nam jim with butterflied chicken

4 x 500g small chickens
⅓ cup (90g) grated palm sugar
2 teaspoons ground cumin
1 teaspoon salt
2 lebanese cucumbers (260g), seeded, sliced thinly
½ cup firmly packed fresh mint leaves
1 cup firmly packed thai basil leaves
1 cup firmly packed fresh coriander leaves

nam jim
2 cloves garlic, chopped coarsely
3 long green chillies, chopped coarsely
2 teaspoons finely chopped coriander root
1 tablespoon fish sauce
1 tablespoon grated palm sugar
2 shallots (50g), chopped coarsely
¼ cup (60ml) lime juice

1 Discard necks from chickens. Using scissors, cut along each side of backbones; discard backbones. Turn chickens skin-side up; press down on breastbone to flatten. Using fork, prick skin several times. Rub each chicken with combined sugar, cumin and salt; stand 5 minutes.

2 Meanwhile, make nam jim.

3 Cook chickens on heated oiled barbecue, uncovered, 10 minutes. Cover; cook, over low heat, about 10 minutes or until chickens are cooked through.

4 Meanwhile, place remaining ingredients in large bowl with 2 tablespoons of the nam jim; toss gently to combine.

5 Serve chickens with salad and remaining nam jim.

nam jim Blend or process ingredients until smooth.

preparation time *15 minutes*
cooking time *25 minutes* serves *4*
nutritional count per serving *20.4g total fat
(6.2g saturated fat); 2167kJ (516 cal);
28.1g carbohydrate; 54g protein; 2.3g fibre*

Nam jim is a generic term for a Thai dipping sauce; most versions include fish sauce and chillies, but the remaining ingredients are up to the cook's discretion.

chicken with rocket and cucumber salad

mini meatloaves italian-style

chicken with rocket and cucumber salad

4 x 500g small chickens
1 tablespoon harissa paste
1 teaspoon finely grated lemon rind
¼ cup (60ml) olive oil
2 teaspoons cumin seeds
1 teaspoon ground coriander
200g yogurt
1 clove garlic, crushed
2 lebanese cucumbers (260g)
150g baby rocket leaves
2 tablespoons lemon juice

1 Discard necks from chickens. Using scissors, cut along each side of backbones; discard backbones. Turn chickens skin-side up; press down on breastbone to flatten.

2 Combine paste, rind and 1 tablespoon of the oil in large bowl; rub mixture all over chickens.

3 Cook chickens on heated oiled barbecue, uncovered, 10 minutes. Cover; cook, over low heat, about 10 minutes or until chickens are cooked through.

4 Meanwhile, dry-fry spices in small frying pan, stirring, until fragrant. Cool 10 minutes. Combine spices with yogurt and garlic in small bowl.

5 Using vegetable peeler, slice cucumber lengthways into ribbons. Combine cucumber in large bowl with rocket, juice and remaining oil.

6 Cut chickens into quarters; serve with yogurt and salad.

preparation time 25 minutes
cooking time 20 minutes serves 4
nutritional count per serving 55.2g total fat
(15.4g saturated fat); 3043kJ (728 cal);
4.9g carbohydrate; 52.8g protein; 1.5g fibre

mini meatloaves italian-style

500g chicken mince
2 cloves garlic, crushed
1 fresh small red thai chilli, chopped finely
⅓ cup (35g) packaged breadcrumbs
1 egg
⅓ cup coarsely chopped fresh basil
⅓ cup (50g) finely chopped sun-dried tomatoes in oil
2 tablespoons roasted pine nuts, chopped coarsely
cooking-oil spray
4 slices prosciutto (60g)

1 Combine chicken, garlic, chilli, breadcrumbs, egg, basil, tomato and nuts in large bowl; shape mixture into four meatloaves.

2 Spray four x 25cm pieces foil with cooking-oil spray. Wrap 1 slice prosciutto around each meatloaf; wrap meatloaves in foil.

3 Cook meatloaves on heated oiled barbecue turning occasionally, about 25 minutes or until cooked through.

4 Remove foil from meatloaves; serve sliced meatloaves with warm potato salad, if desired.

preparation time 15 minutes
cooking time 30 minutes serves 4
nutritional count per serving 19.3g total fat
(7.2g saturated fat); 1467kJ (351 cal);
10.8g carbohydrate; 32.1g protein; 2.9g fibre

piri piri chicken thigh fillets

4 fresh long red chillies, chopped coarsely
1 teaspoon dried chilli flakes
2 cloves garlic, quartered
1 teaspoon sea salt
2 tablespoons olive oil
1 tablespoon cider vinegar
2 teaspoons brown sugar
8 x 125g chicken thigh fillets

1   Using mortar and pestle, grind fresh chilli, chilli flakes, garlic and salt to make piri piri paste.

2   Combine paste with oil, vinegar, sugar and chicken in medium bowl.

3   Cook chicken on heated oiled barbecue until cooked through. Serve with lime, if desired.

preparation time *10 minutes*
cooking time *15 minutes* serves *4*
nutritional count per serving *27.2g total fat
(6.8g saturated fat); 1822kJ (436 cal);
1.8g carbohydrate; 46.6g protein; 0.3g fibre*

Piri piri is a spicy Afro-Portuguese chilli paste.

spiced chicken with tomato chilli sauce

2 teaspoons olive oil
¼ cup (60ml) lemon juice
1 teaspoon ground cumin
2 teaspoons sweet paprika
8 x 125g chicken thigh fillets

tomato chilli sauce
¼ cup (55g) brown sugar
¼ cup (60ml) red wine vinegar
2 fresh long red chillies, chopped coarsely
4 large egg tomatoes (360g), chopped coarsely

1   Make tomato chilli sauce.

2   Meanwhile, combine oil, juice, spices and chicken in medium bowl.

3   Cook chicken on heated oiled barbecue until cooked through. Serve chicken with sauce.

tomato chilli sauce Combine sugar and vinegar in medium saucepan; cook, stirring, over low heat, until sugar dissolves. Add chilli and tomato; bring to the boil. Reduce heat; simmer, uncovered, 15 minutes. Drain sauce over small bowl; reserve solids. Return liquid to pan; bring to the boil. Boil, uncovered, until liquid is reduced by half. Return tomato solids to pan; stir over heat until sauce is hot.

preparation time *10 minutes*
cooking time *25 minutes* serves *4*
nutritional count per serving *20.4g total fat
(5.8g saturated fat); 1747kJ (418 cal);
10.8 carbohydrate; 47.6g protein; 1.1g fibre*

piri piri chicken thigh fillets

spiced chicken with tomato chilli sauce

chicken wings and green mango salad

10cm stick fresh lemon grass (20g), chopped finely
1 long green chilli, chopped finely
3 cloves garlic, crushed
10 fresh kaffir lime leaves, shredded finely
16 chicken wings (1.5kg)
2 small green mangoes (600g)
1 large carrot (180g)
1 lebanese cucumber (130g)
1 medium red capsicum (200g), sliced thinly
2 green onions, sliced thinly

sweet and sour dressing
2 tablespoons fish sauce
2 tablespoons lime juice
2 tablespoons grated palm sugar
1 tablespoon white vinegar
1 tablespoon water

1 Make sweet and sour dressing.

2 Combine lemon grass, chilli, garlic, about half the lime leaves and 2 tablespoons of the dressing in medium bowl; add chicken, toss to coat in marinade. Cover chicken and remaining dressing separately; refrigerate overnight.

3 Drain chicken; discard marinade. Cook chicken on heated oiled barbecue until cooked through.

4 Meanwhile, use vegetable peeler to finely slice mangoes, carrot and cucumber into ribbons. Place in medium bowl with capsicum, remaining lime leaves and remaining dressing; toss gently to combine.

5 Serve chicken with salad; sprinkle with onion.

sweet and sour dressing Combine ingredients in screw-top jar; shake well.

preparation time *20 minutes (plus refrigeration time)*
cooking time *15 minutes* serves *4*
nutritional count per serving *13g total fat (4.1g saturated fat); 1919kJ (459 cal); 25.3g carbohydrate; 57.4g protein; 4.3g fibre*

Sour and crunchy, green mangoes are just immature fruit that can be eaten as a vegetable in salads, salsas, curries and stir-fries. They will keep, wrapped in plastic, in the fridge for up to two weeks.

maple chicken, shallot and kumara skewers

1 large kumara (500g), cut into 2cm pieces
660g chicken thigh fillets, cut into 3cm pieces
12 shallots (300g), halved
2 tablespoons maple syrup
1 tablespoon cider vinegar
1 teaspoon dijon mustard

1 Boil, steam or microwave kumara until tender; drain. Thread kumara, chicken and shallot, alternately, onto eight skewers.

2 Combine syrup, vinegar and mustard in small bowl.

3 Cook skewers on heated oiled barbecue, covered with foil, 10 minutes. Uncover, brush skewers all over with syrup mixture. Turn; cook skewers, brushing occasionally with syrup mixture, about 5 minutes or until chicken is cooked through.

4 Skewers can be served with a spinach pecan salad.

preparation time *15 minutes*
cooking time *20 minutes* serves *4*
nutritional count per serving *12.2g total fat (3.6g saturated fat); 1484kJ (355 cal); 26.4g carbohydrate; 33.8g protein; 2.7g fibre*

You need 8 skewers for this recipe. If using bamboo skewers, soak them in cold water for at least an hour before using to prevent them from splintering and scorching during cooking.

chicken with salsa verde and kipfler mash

8 chicken thigh fillets (880g)
600g kipfler potatoes, unpeeled
50g butter, chopped

salsa verde
½ cup coarsely chopped fresh flat-leaf parsley
¼ cup coarsely chopped fresh mint
⅓ cup (80ml) olive oil
½ cup (125ml) lemon juice
¼ cup (50g) rinsed, drained capers, chopped coarsely
8 drained anchovy fillets, chopped finely
2 cloves garlic, crushed

1 Make salsa verde.

2 Place ⅓ cup of the salsa verde in medium bowl; add chicken, turn to coat in salsa marinade.

3 Cook chicken on heated oiled barbecue until browned both sides and cooked through.

4 Meanwhile, boil, steam or microwave potatoes until tender; drain. Using potato masher, crush potatoes roughly in large bowl with butter.

5 Serve chicken with potato; top with remaining salsa verde.

salsa verde Combine ingredients in small bowl.

preparation time *15 minutes*
cooking time *25 minutes* serves *4*
nutritional count per serving *45.3g total fat (14.3g saturated fat); 2897kJ (693 cal); 22.1g carbohydrate; 47.2g protein; 3.5g fibre*

maple chicken, shallot and kumara skewers

chicken with salsa verde and kipfler mash

turkey steaks with green olive and tomato relish

1kg potatoes
4 turkey steaks (800g)
1 teaspoon sea salt
½ teaspoon cracked black pepper

green olive and tomato relish
1 tablespoon extra virgin olive oil
1 small red onion (100g), chopped finely
1 clove garlic, crushed
2 large green tomatoes (440g), chopped finely
2 cups (240g) seeded green olives, chopped finely
2 tablespoons white sugar
¼ cup (60ml) cider vinegar
2 tablespoons rinsed, drained capers, chopped finely
⅓ cup finely chopped fresh flat-leaf parsley

1 Make green olive and tomato relish.

2 Meanwhile, cut potatoes into 1cm slices; cook on heated oiled grill plate until tender.

3 Sprinkle turkey with salt and pepper; cook on heated oiled barbecue until cooked through. Serve turkey with potato and relish.

green olive and tomato relish Heat oil in medium saucepan; cook onion and garlic, stirring, until onion softens. Add tomato, olives, sugar and vinegar; cook, stirring occasionally, 10 minutes. Remove from heat; stir in capers and parsley.

preparation time *10 minutes*
cooking time *30 minutes* serves *4*
nutritional count per serving *15.7g total fat (3.2g saturated fat); 2174kJ (520 cal); 41.6g carbohydrate; 48.4g protein; 8.1g fibre*

The relish can be stored, covered, in the refrigerator for up to two weeks.

indochine chicken salad

2 teaspoons five-spice powder
¼ cup (60ml) mirin
2 tablespoons chinese cooking wine
2 cloves garlic, crushed
4 x 200g chicken thigh cutlets
125g rice vermicelli
150g snow peas, sliced thinly
1 cup (80g) bean sprouts
2 green onions, sliced thinly
½ cup coarsely chopped fresh coriander
¼ cup loosely packed fresh vietnamese mint leaves
2 medium carrots (240g), cut into matchsticks

lime dressing
⅓ cup (80ml) lime juice
⅓ cup (80ml) mirin
2 cloves garlic, crushed
1 tablespoon grated palm sugar

1   Combine five-spice, mirin, cooking wine and garlic in large bowl; add chicken, turn to coat in marinade. Cover; refrigerate 3 hours or overnight.

2   Make lime dressing.

3   Cook chicken on heated oiled barbecue turning and brushing occasionally with marinade, about 40 minutes or until cooked through.

4   Meanwhile, place vermicelli in large heatproof bowl, cover with boiling water; stand until just tender, drain. Rinse vermicelli under cold water; drain.

5   Place vermicelli and dressing in large bowl with remaining ingredients; toss salad to combine. Serve with chicken.

lime dressing Combine ingredients in screw-top jar; shake well.

preparation time *25 minutes (plus refrigeration time)*
cooking time *40 minutes* serves *4*
nutritional count per serving *20.5g total fat
(6.6g saturated fat); 1668kJ (399 cal);
17.2g carbohydrate; 26.9g protein; 4.2g fibre*

cajun chicken with spicy tomato salsa

6 x 500g small chickens
2 tablespoons olive oil
1 small brown onion (80g), grated coarsely
2 cloves garlic, crushed
2 tablespoons sweet paprika
2 teaspoons ground cinnamon
2 teaspoons ground fennel
2 teaspoons dried oregano

spicy tomato salsa
6 large egg tomatoes (540g), halved
1 tablespoon olive oil
1 medium brown onion (150g), chopped finely
2 cloves garlic, crushed
1 tablespoon sweet paprika
1 teaspoon smoked paprika
1 tablespoon red wine vinegar
1 fresh long red chilli, chopped finely

1 Discard necks from chickens. Using scissors, cut along each side of backbones; discard backbones. Turn chickens skin-side up; press down on breastbone to flatten.

2 Rub chickens all over with combined remaining ingredients.

3 Cook chickens on heated oiled barbecue 10 minutes. Cover; cook, over low heat, about 10 minutes or until chickens are cooked through.

4 Meanwhile, make spicy tomato salsa.

5 Cut chickens into quarters; serve with spicy tomato salsa.

spicy tomato salsa Cook tomato on heated oiled barbecue, turning, until softened; chop tomato coarsely. Heat oil in medium saucepan; cook onion and garlic, stirring, until onion softens. Add spices; cook, stirring, until fragrant. Stir in tomato, vinegar and chilli; cook, uncovered, stirring occasionally, about 20 minutes or until salsa thickens.

preparation time *20 minutes*
cooking time *1 hour* serves *6*
nutritional count per serving *48.8g total fat (13.6g saturated fat); 2746kJ (657 cal); 4g carbohydrate; 50.6g protein; 2.1g fibre*

guava-glazed turkey salad with mandarin

⅓ cup (80ml) dry sherry
1 tablespoon golden syrup
1 tablespoon dijon mustard
1 clove garlic, crushed
1 small brown onion (80g), chopped finely
⅓ cup (80ml) guava nectar
1.5kg turkey breast fillets
5 medium mandarins (1kg)
300g curly endive, trimmed
⅓ cup coarsely chopped fresh flat-leaf parsley

mandarin dressing
2 tablespoons mandarin juice
1 teaspoon dijon mustard
1 teaspoon white wine vinegar
2 tablespoons guava nectar

1   Combine sherry, syrup, mustard, garlic, onion and nectar in small saucepan; simmer, uncovered, about 10 minutes or until mixture thickens slightly. Stand 5 minutes.

2   Combine sherry mixture in large bowl with turkey. Cook turkey on heated oiled barbecue turning and brushing occasionally with sherry mixture, about 40 minutes or until cooked through. Cover turkey; stand 10 minutes then slice thickly.

3   Meanwhile, segment mandarins over large bowl.

4   Make mandarin dressing.

5   Combine turkey in bowl with mandarin, endive, parsley and dressing; toss gently.

mandarin dressing Combine ingredients in screw-top jar; shake well.

preparation time 25 minutes
cooking time 50 minutes serves 6
nutritional count per serving 8.7g total fat
(2g saturated fat); 1672kJ (400 cal);
17.8g carbohydrate; 56.4g protein; 4.1g fibre

burgers italian-style

500g chicken mince
¼ cup (35g) sun-dried tomatoes in oil, drained, chopped finely
1 tablespoon finely chopped fresh basil
1 egg
1 cup (70g) stale breadcrumbs
3 cloves garlic, crushed
4 slices pancetta (60g)
1 loaf focaccia bread (440g)
½ cup (150g) mayonnaise
40g baby rocket leaves
120g bocconcini cheese, sliced thickly

1   Combine chicken in large bowl with tomato, basil, egg, breadcrumbs and about a third of the garlic; shape mixture into four patties.

2   Cook patties on heated oiled barbecue until browned and cooked through.

3   Cook pancetta on heated oiled barbecue until crisp; drain on absorbent paper.

4   Quarter focaccia; slice each square in half horizontally. Toast cut sides on heated oiled barbecue.

5   Combine mayonnaise with remaining garlic; spread on focaccia bases. Sandwich rocket, burgers, pancetta and cheese between focaccia quarters.

preparation time 20 minutes
cooking time 20 minutes serves 4
nutritional count per serving 34.9g total fat
(9.3g saturated fat); 3357kJ (803 cal);
71.5g carbohydrate; 47.6g protein; 5.6g fibre

guava-glazed turkey salad with mandarin

burgers italian-style

rosemary and prosciutto chicken legs with creamy risoni

8 stalks fresh rosemary
8 chicken drumsticks (1.5kg)
8 slices prosciutto (120g)
1 cup (220g) risoni
1 tablespoon olive oil
1 medium brown onion (150g), chopped finely
1 clove garlic, crushed
300ml cream
¼ teaspoon dried chilli flakes
250g cherry tomatoes, halved
1 tablespoon fresh lemon thyme leaves

1 Press one rosemary stalk onto each drumstick; firmly wrap one prosciutto slice around each to hold in place.

2 Cook chicken on heated oiled barbecue, uncovered, until browned all over. Place chicken in covered barbecue; cook, using indirect heat, following manufacturer's instructions, about 40 minutes or until cooked through.

3 Meanwhile, cook risoni in large saucepan of boiling water until tender; drain. Rinse under cold water; drain.

4 Heat oil in large frying pan; cook onion and garlic, stirring, until onion softens. Add cream and chilli; simmer, uncovered, until mixture thickens. Add risoni, tomato and half the thyme; cook, stirring, until tomato just softens. Serve with chicken; sprinkle with remaining thyme.

preparation time *30 minutes*
cooking time *45 minutes* serves *4*
nutritional count per serving *60.4g total fat (29.2g saturated fat); 3783kJ (509 cal); 42.6g carbohydrate; 47.3g protein; 3.4g fibre*

Risoni is a very small, rice-shaped pasta.

honey chicken with fennel and celery slaw

2 tablespoons honey
2 teaspoons dijon mustard
4 x 200g chicken breast fillets

fennel and celery slaw
2 medium fennel bulbs (600g)
3 trimmed celery stalks (300g), sliced thinly
¼ cup coarsely chopped fresh flat-leaf parsley
2 teaspoons dijon mustard
2 tablespoons lemon juice
2 tablespoons light sour cream
2 cloves garlic, crushed
¼ cup (75g) mayonnaise

1 Combine honey and mustard in small bowl. Brush chicken both sides with half the honey mixture; cook on heated oiled barbecue until cooked through, brushing with remaining honey mixture.

2 Meanwhile, make fennel and celery slaw.

3 Serve chicken with slaw; sprinkle with reserved fennel fronds.

fennel and celery slaw Trim fennel, reserving about 1 tablespoon of the fronds. Slice fennel thinly; combine with celery and parsley in large bowl. Combine remaining ingredients in small bowl, pour over slaw mixture; toss gently to combine.

preparation time *20 minutes*
cooking time *30 minutes* serves *4*
nutritional information per serving *19.4g total fat (5.4g saturated fat); 1860kJ (445 cal); 20.2g carbohydrate; 45.1g protein; 4.4g fibre*

lemon thyme chicken

6 cloves garlic, sliced thickly
3 shallots (75g), chopped finely
½ cup (125ml) chicken stock
20g butter, softened
1 tablespoon finely chopped fresh lemon thyme
1.6kg chicken
600g kipfler potatoes, halved lengthways
340g asparagus, trimmed
1 medium lemon, quartered
1 tablespoon olive oil

1 Place garlic, shallot and stock in small saucepan; bring to the boil. Reduce heat; simmer, uncovered, about 20 minutes or until garlic is soft and liquid is almost evaporated. Cool 5 minutes; stir in butter and thyme.

2 Using kitchen scissors, cut along each side of backbone; discard backbone. Place chicken, skin-side up, on board. Using heel of hand, press down on breastbone to flatten chicken. Make a pocket between chicken and skin; push thyme mixture under skin.

3 Cook chicken, skin-side down, in covered barbecue, using indirect heat, following manufacturer's instructions, 15 minutes. Turn chicken; cook, covered, about 35 minutes or until cooked through. Cover chicken; stand 15 minutes.

4 Boil, steam or microwave potato until just tender; drain. Cook potato, asparagus and lemon, on heated oiled barbecue, uncovered, brushing with the oil, until browned.

5 Cut chicken into pieces; serve with potato, asparagus and lemon.

preparation time *25 minutes (plus standing time)*
cooking time *1 hour* serves *4*
nutritional count per serving *41.4g total fat (13.5g saturated fat); 2776kJ (664 cal); 22.8g carbohydrate; 46.7g protein; 5.4g fibre*

honey chicken with fennel and celery slaw

lemon thyme chicken

kofta with date chutney and spiced eggplant

¼ cup (50g) brown rice
1 tablespoon olive oil
1 small brown onion (80g), chopped finely
1 clove garlic, crushed
1 long green chilli, chopped finely
500g chicken mince
½ cup firmly packed fresh coriander leaves
1 egg

spiced eggplant
1 tablespoon olive oil
2 teaspoons cumin seeds
2 teaspoons yellow mustard seeds
6 baby eggplants (360g), sliced thickly
1 medium brown onion (150g), sliced thinly
1 clove garlic, crushed
½ cup (125ml) water
420g can chickpeas, rinsed, drained
¼ cup firmly packed fresh coriander leaves

date chutney
½ cup (70g) seeded dried dates, chopped finely
¼ cup (60ml) orange juice
¼ cup (60ml) water

1 Cook rice in large saucepan of boiling water, uncovered, until just tender; drain. Rinse under cold water; drain, cool.

2 Heat oil in small frying pan; add onion, garlic and chilli. Cook, stirring, until onion softens; cool. Process onion mixture with chicken, rice, coriander and egg until smooth.

3 Shape chicken mixture into 12 patties. Place patties on tray, cover; refrigerate until required.

4 Make spiced eggplant. Make date chutney.

5 Cook patties on heated oiled barbecue until browned both sides and cooked through. Serve kofta with eggplant; top with date chutney.

spiced eggplant Heat oil in medium saucepan; fry seeds, over low heat, until fragrant. Add eggplant, onion and garlic; cook, stirring, about 5 minutes or until just softened. Add the water and chickpeas; bring to the boil. Reduce heat; simmer, uncovered, about 15 minutes or until mixture thickens. Remove from heat; cool 10 minutes then stir in coriander.

date chutney Combine ingredients in small saucepan; bring to the boil. Reduce heat; simmer, uncovered, 5 minutes. Cool 5 minutes; blend or process until smooth.

preparation time *30 minutes* (plus cooling time)
cooking time *45 minutes* serves *4*
nutritional count per serving *17.8g total fat
(3.5g saturated fat); 1935kJ (463 cal);
37.1g carbohydrate; 35.4g protein; 8.6g fibre*

sichuan duck with watercress and snow pea salad

piri piri quail

sichuan duck with snow pea salad

½ cup (125ml) chinese cooking wine
2 tablespoons light soy sauce
2 cloves garlic, crushed
4cm piece fresh ginger (20g), sliced thinly
1 teaspoon sesame oil
4 duck marylands (1.5kg)
2 teaspoons sichuan peppercorns
1 teaspoon sea salt
100g watercress, trimmed
150g snow peas, trimmed, sliced thinly
1 small red onion (100g), sliced thinly
½ cup loosely packed fresh coriander leaves
½ cup (70g) roasted unsalted peanuts,
    chopped coarsely
2 tablespoons lime juice
1 tablespoon peanut oil
1 clove garlic, crushed, extra

1 Combine cooking wine, sauce, garlic, ginger and sesame oil in large bowl with duck. Cover; refrigerate 3 hours or overnight.

2 Drain duck; discard marinade.

3 Dry-fry peppercorns in small frying pan until fragrant. Crush peppercorns and salt using mortar and pestle; press mixture onto duck skin.

4 Cook duck on heated oiled barbecue turning halfway through cooking time, about 40 minutes or until cooked.

5 Meanwhile, combine remaining ingredients in large bowl; serve with duck.

preparation time *20 minutes (plus refrigeration time)*
cooking time *40 minutes* serves *4*
nutritional count per serving *92.9g total fat*
(25.6g saturated fat); 4314kJ (1032 cal);
6.5g carbohydrate; 35.1g protein; 4.1g fibre

piri piri quail

6 quails (1kg)
⅓ cup (80ml) piri piri sauce
4 baby eggplants (240g), halved
4 small zucchini (360g), halved
200g yellow grape tomatoes
1 green onion, sliced thinly

chilli dressing
2 tablespoons piri piri sauce
1 clove garlic
⅓ cup (100g) mayonnaise

1 Make chilli dressing.

2 Discard necks from quails. Using scissors, cut along each side of backbones; discard backbones. Cut quails in half; combine in medium bowl with sauce.

3 Cook quail on heated oiled barbecue about 25 minutes or until cooked through.

4 Meanwhile, cook eggplant and zucchini on heated oiled barbecue until browned both sides.

5 Cook tomatoes on heated oiled barbecue until softened.

6 Serve quail with vegetables and dressing; sprinkle with onion.

chilli dressing Combine ingredients in small bowl.

preparation time *15 minutes*
cooking time *25 minutes* serves *4*
nutritional count per serving *22.3g total fat*
(4.6g saturated fat); 1442kJ (345 cal);
8.9g carbohydrate; 25.8g protein; 3.8g fibre

Piri piri sauce is a spicy Afro-Portuguese chilli sauce available from Middle-Eastern food stores and most major supermarkets.

vegetables

mushrooms with herb butter, page 174

Vegetables grill beautifully and are a fantastic addition to a barbecued meal. Slice large vegies thinly, then spray or brush with a little oil.

mushrooms
with herb butter

80g butter, melted
1 teaspoon grated lime rind
1 tablespoon lime juice
1 tablespoon finely chopped fresh flat-leaf parsley
1 tablespoon finely chopped fresh basil
6 large flat mushrooms (840g)

1 Combine butter, rind, juice and herbs in small bowl.

2 Cook mushrooms on heated oiled barbecue, brushing with half the butter mixture, until mushrooms are just tender and browned. Serve with remaining butter.

preparation time *10 minutes*
cooking time *10 minutes* serves *6*
nutritional count per serving *11.4g total fat*
(7.2g saturated fat); 548kJ (131 cal);
0.6g carbohydrate; 5.2g protein; 3.6g fibre

barbecued
kumara slices

2 large kumara (1kg), cut into 1cm slices
1 clove garlic, crushed
2 tablespoons golden syrup
2 teaspoons balsamic vinegar
¼ teaspoon ground cinnamon

1 Boil, steam or microwave kumara until just tender; drain.

2 Cook kumara on heated oiled barbecue until browned. Turn, brush with combined garlic, golden syrup, vinegar and cinnamon; cook until browned and tender.

preparation time *15 minutes*
cooking time *25 minutes* serves *6*
nutritional count per serving *0.2g total fat*
(0g saturated fat); 443kJ (106 cal);
23.3g carbohydrate; 2.2g protein; 2.1g fibre

barbecued kumara slices

1 Cook asparagus on heated oiled barbecue about 5 minutes or until tender.

2 Make toppings.

3 Arrange asparagus in three piles on serving platter. Top each pile with one of the following toppings.

preparation time *10 minutes*
cooking time *10 minutes* serves *4*

asparagus with three toppings

600g asparagus, trimmed

anchovies and garlic
2 tablespoons extra virgin olive oil
1 clove garlic, sliced thinly
3 drained anchovies, chopped coarsely

parmesan butter
25g butter
2 tablespoons parmesan cheese flakes

balsamic dressing
2 tablespoons extra virgin olive oil
3 teaspoons balsamic vinegar
1 medium tomato (150g), peeled,
    seeded, chopped finely
1 tablespoon small basil leaves

anchovies and garlic Heat oil in small frying pan; cook garlic and anchovy until browned lightly. Sprinkle over asparagus.

nutritional count per serving *18.8g total fat (2.7g saturated fat); 786kJ (188 cal); 1.6g carbohydrate; 3.8g protein; 1.8g fibre*

parmesan butter Melt butter in small saucepan. Pour over asparagus; sprinkle with cheese.

nutritional count per serving *10.6g total fat (6.9g saturated fat); 506kJ (121 cal); 1.5g carbohydrate; 5.2g protein; 1.5g fibre*

balsamic dressing Combine ingredients in small bowl. Spoon over asparagus.

nutritional count per serving *18.4g total fat (2.6g saturated fat); 790kJ (189 cal); 2.8g carbohydrate; 3.3g protein; 2.5g fibre*

from top: anchovies and garlic, parmesan butter, balsamic dressing

eggplant, fetta and capsicum stack with mesclun

sesame banana chillies, corn and green onions

eggplant, fetta and capsicum stack with mesclun

2 medium red capsicums (400g)
¼ cup (60ml) olive oil
2 tablespoons lemon juice
1 clove garlic, crushed
1 large eggplant (500g)
1 cup (150g) drained sun-dried tomatoes in oil,
    chopped coarsely
¼ cup (50g) seeded kalamata olives,
    chopped coarsely
½ cup loosely packed fresh basil leaves, torn
100g mesclun
2 tablespoons red wine vinegar
200g fetta cheese, cut into 8 slices
1 tablespoon small whole fresh basil leaves

1 Quarter capsicums; discard seeds and membranes. Cook capsicum on heated oiled barbecue, skin-side down, until skin blisters and blackens. Cover with paper or plastic wrap for 5 minutes then peel away skin.

2 Meanwhile, combine 2 tablespoons of the oil in small bowl with juice and garlic. Cut eggplant lengthways into 8 slices; discard skin-covered end pieces. Brush slices, both sides, with oil mixture; cook on heated barbecue, brushing occasionally with oil mixture, until just tender.

3 Combine tomato, olives and torn basil in small bowl. Place mesclun in medium bowl; drizzle with combined vinegar and remaining oil, toss gently.

4 Place 1 slice of the eggplant on each serving plate; top each with 2 slices of the cheese, 2 pieces of the capsicum and remaining eggplant slices. Top with tomato mixture, sprinkle with whole basil leaves; serve with mesclun.

preparation time *15 minutes*
cooking time *15 minutes* serves *4*
nutritional count per serving *27.8g total fat*
(9.8g saturated fat); 1781kJ (426 cal);
23.3g carbohydrate; 16.4g protein; 10.2g fibre

sesame banana chillies, corn and green onions

12 banana chillies (1kg)
350g baby corn
300g green onions, trimmed
2 teaspoons sesame oil
1 teaspoon sesame seeds, toasted

1 Cook chillies, corn and onion on heated oiled barbecue until browned and tender.

2 Transfer vegetables to serving platter, drizzle with oil; sprinkle with seeds before serving.

preparation time *5 minutes*
cooking time *10 minutes* serves *6*
nutritional count per serving *2.9g total fat*
(0.3g saturated fat); 497kJ (119 cal);
15.4g carbohydrate; 4.7g protein; 6.1g fibre

The vegetables are best cooked just before serving.

barbecued kipflers

12 kipfler potatoes (1.5kg), unpeeled
2 tablespoons fresh oregano leaves
¼ cup loosely packed fresh thyme leaves
1 tablespoon coarsely grated lemon rind
2 cloves garlic, crushed
⅓ cup (80ml) olive oil
¼ cup (60ml) lemon juice

1 Boil, steam or microwave potatoes until tender; drain. Halve potatoes lengthways.

2 Combine herbs, rind, garlic and oil in large bowl; add potato, toss to coat in mixture. Cook potato on heated oiled barbecue about 15 minutes or until browned and tender.

3 Serve potato drizzled with juice.

preparation time *10 minutes*
cooking time *30 minutes* serves *8*
nutritional count per serving *9.3g total fat (1.3g saturated fat); 878kJ (210 cal); 24.9g carbohydrate; 4.6g protein; 3.9g fibre*

vegetable salad

1 large red onion (300g)
8 medium egg tomatoes (600g)
8 baby eggplant (480g)
4 medium zucchini (480g)
4 medium yellow patty-pan squash (120g), halved
2 medium red capsicums (400g), sliced thickly

balsamic dressing
¼ cup (60ml) extra virgin olive oil
¼ cup (60ml) balsamic vinegar
1 clove garlic, crushed

1 Make balsamic dressing.

2 Cut onion and tomatoes into eight wedges each; thinly slice eggplant and zucchini lengthways.

3 Cook onion, tomato, eggplant, zucchini, squash and capsicum, in batches, on heated oiled barbecue until vegetables are browned and just tender.

4 Combine vegetables in large bowl, drizzle with dressing; toss gently.

balsamic dressing Combine ingredients in screw-top jar; shake well.

preparation time *25 minutes*
cooking time *30 minutes* serves *8*
nutritional count per serving *7.4g total fat (1g saturated fat); 518kJ (124 cal); 8.5g carbohydrate; 3.8g protein; 4.8g fibre*

barbecued kipflers

vegetable salad

asian vegetables

marinated mixed mushrooms

asian vegetables

400g baby buk choy, trimmed, halved lengthways
2 tablespoons peanut oil
175g broccolini, halved
100g snow peas, trimmed
200g baby corn, halved lengthways
2 tablespoons mirin
1 tablespoon vegetarian oyster sauce
1 tablespoon light soy sauce
1 clove garlic, crushed
1 teaspoon white sugar
½ teaspoon sesame oil

1 Boil, steam or microwave buk choy until wilted; drain. Brush with half the peanut oil; cook buk choy on heated barbecue until tender.

2 Combine broccolini, peas and corn in large bowl with remaining peanut oil; mix well. Cook vegetables, in batches, on heated barbecue until tender.

3 Meanwhile, combine mirin, sauces, garlic, sugar and sesame oil in same large bowl; add vegetables, mix well.

preparation time *10 minutes*
cooking time *10 minutes* serves *4*
nutritional count per serving *10.7g total fat (1.8g saturated fat); 811kJ (194 cal); 13.4g carbohydrate; 6.5g protein; 6.1g fibre*

Vegetarian oyster sauce is made from blended mushrooms and soy sauce, and is available from health food stores and some supermarkets.

marinated mixed mushrooms

2 cloves garlic, crushed
4cm piece fresh ginger (20g), grated
⅓ cup (80ml) light soy sauce
2 tablespoons mirin
2 tablespoons sake
2 tablespoons peanut oil
1 tablespoon white sugar
200g oyster mushrooms
200g shiitake mushrooms
200g button mushrooms
200g swiss brown mushrooms
200g enoki mushrooms
4 green onions, sliced diagonally

1 Combine garlic, ginger, sauce, mirin, sake, oil and sugar in large bowl; add mushrooms, mix gently. Cover; refrigerate 2 hours.

2 Drain mushrooms; reserve marinade in bowl.

3 Cook mushrooms on heated oiled barbecue until tender. Combine mushrooms and onion in bowl with reserved marinade.

preparation time *15 minutes (plus refrigeration time)*
cooking time *10 minutes* serves *4*
nutritional count per serving *9.8g total fat (1.7g saturated fat); 890kJ (213 cal); 14.9g carbohydrate; 9.2g protein; 7.7g fibre*

chilli, tofu and vegetable kebabs

25 fresh small red thai chillies
⅔ cup (160ml) olive oil
2 teaspoons grated lemon rind
⅓ cup (80ml) lemon juice
1 tablespoon finely chopped fresh oregano
1 tablespoon finely chopped fresh dill
2 cloves garlic, crushed
300g packet firm tofu, drained
1 large red onion (300g)
2 medium zucchini (250g)
6 medium yellow patty-pan squash (180g)
12 large cherry tomatoes (250g)

1   Remove and discard seeds from one of the chillies; chop finely.

2   Combine oil, rind, juice, herbs, garlic and chopped chilli in screw-top jar; shake well.

3   Cut tofu into 12 even pieces; cut onion into 12 wedges. Cut zucchini into 12 pieces and cut each squash in half.

4   Thread one chilli then a piece of zucchini, tofu, tomato, onion, squash and another chilli onto a skewer. Repeat with remaining skewers, chilli, tofu and vegetables.

5   Cook kebabs on heated oiled barbecue, brushing with half the oil mixture, until vegetables are browned both sides and just tender, turning only once as the tofu is delicate and breaks easily.

6   Serve kebabs with remaining oil mixture.

preparation time *30 minutes*
cooking time *15 minutes* serves *4*
nutritional count per serving *42g total fat
(5.9g saturated fat); 1981kJ (474 cal);
10.1g carbohydrate; 12.8g protein; 5.9g fibre*

You need 12 bamboo skewers for this recipe. Soak them in water for an hour before use to prevent them from splintering or scorching during cooking. The chillies we used are fiery hot – warn your guests before they eat them.

vegetables with garlic rosemary dressing

asparagus with tomato

vegetables with garlic rosemary dressing

1 medium red capsicum (200g)
1 medium yellow capsicum (200g)
¼ cup (60ml) olive oil
1 clove garlic, crushed
1 teaspoon finely grated lemon rind
2 teaspoons finely chopped fresh rosemary
1 medium red onion (170g), cut into wedges
2 small leeks (400g), trimmed, cut into 2cm pieces
1 medium eggplant (300g), sliced thickly
2 medium zucchini (240g), sliced thickly
4 flat mushrooms (320g), quartered
3 cloves garlic, unpeeled
⅓ cup (100g) mayonnaise
1 tablespoon lemon juice

1 Quarter capsicums, discard seeds and membranes. Cook capsicum on heated oiled barbecue until skin blisters and blackens. Cover capsicum pieces in plastic or paper for 5 minutes then peel away skin; slice capsicum thickly.

2 Combine oil, crushed garlic, rind and half the rosemary in small bowl.

3 Brush onion, leek, eggplant, zucchini, mushrooms and unpeeled garlic with oil mixture; cook vegetables, in batches, on heated oiled barbecue until tender.

4 Squeeze cooked garlic into small jug; discard skins. Whisk in remaining rosemary, mayonnaise and juice. Serve vegetables with dressing.

preparation time *30 minutes*
cooking time *30 minutes* serves *4*
nutritional count per serving *22.8g total fat
(2.9g saturated fat); 1325kJ (317 cal);
16.9g carbohydrate; 7.9g protein; 8.4g fibre*

asparagus with tomato

¼ cup (60ml) olive oil
¼ cup (60ml) white wine vinegar
2 teaspoons fresh lemon thyme leaves
2 cloves garlic, crushed
2 large red onions (600g), cut into wedges
680g asparagus, trimmed, halved widthways
250g cherry tomatoes, halved

1 Combine oil, vinegar, thyme, garlic and onion in large bowl. Drain onion; reserve vinegar mixture in bowl.

2 Cook onion on heated oiled barbecue until soft and browned lightly.

3 Cook asparagus and tomato, in batches, on heated oiled barbecue until tender.

4 Combine vegetables in large bowl with reserved vinegar mixture.

preparation time *10 minutes*
cooking time *20 minutes serves 4*
nutritional count per serving *14.1g total fat
(1.9g saturated fat); 895kJ (214 cal);
12g carbohydrate; 6.8g protein; 5.8g fibre*

You need four bunches of asparagus for this recipe.

fennel, orange and red onion with quinoa

5 small fennel bulbs (1kg), trimmed,
    quartered lengthways
1 large red onion (300g), cut into thick wedges
2 tablespoons olive oil
2 cups (500ml) water
1 cup (170g) quinoa
½ cup (125ml) white wine vinegar
¼ cup coarsely chopped fresh dill
1 medium orange (240g), segmented
1 cup firmly packed fresh flat-leaf parsley leaves

1   Cook fennel and onion on heated oiled barbecue until vegetables are just tender, brushing with about half of the oil occasionally.

2   Meanwhile, bring the water to the boil in small saucepan. Add quinoa; reduce heat, simmer, covered, about 10 minutes or until water is absorbed. Drain.

3   Place fennel, onion and quinoa in large bowl with vinegar, dill, orange, parsley and remaining oil; toss gently.

preparation time *20 minutes*
cooking time *30 minutes* serves *4*
nutritional count per serving *10.2g total fat
(1.4g saturated fat); 1208kJ (289 cal);
39.7g carbohydrate; 8.1g protein; 14g fibre*

Quinoa, pronounced keen-wa, is the seed of a leafy plant similar to spinach. Like corn, rice, buckwheat and millet, quinoa is gluten-free and thought to be safe for consumption by people with coeliac disease. Its cooking qualities are similar to rice, and it has a delicate, slightly nutty taste and chewy texture. You can buy it in most health food stores and some delicatessens. Keep it sealed in a glass jar in the refrigerator because it spoils easily.

piri piri vegetables with polenta

4 baby eggplants (240g), sliced thickly
2 medium red onions (340g), cut into wedges
2 large flat mushrooms (200g), sliced thickly
4 large egg tomatoes (360g), quartered, seeded
3 large zucchini (450g), sliced thickly lengthways
1 litre (4 cups) water
1 cup (170g) polenta
50g butter
½ cup (40g) finely grated parmesan cheese

piri piri marinade
4 fresh small red thai chillies, halved
⅓ cup (80ml) red wine vinegar
2 cloves garlic, quartered
⅓ cup (80ml) olive oil

1   Make piri piri marinade.

2   Toss eggplant, onion, mushrooms, tomato and zucchini in large bowl with marinade; cover, refrigerate 3 hours or overnight.

3   Meanwhile, grease deep 19cm-square cake pan. Place the water in medium saucepan; bring to the boil. Gradually add polenta to liquid, stirring constantly. Reduce heat; cook, stirring, about 10 minutes or until polenta thickens. Stir in butter and cheese then spread polenta into prepared pan; cool 10 minutes. Cover; refrigerate overnight.

4   Turn polenta onto board; trim edges. Cut polenta into quarters then into triangles. Cook polenta and drained vegetables on heated oiled barbecue about 10 minutes or until polenta is browned lightly and vegetables are tender. Serve polenta with vegetables.

piri piri marinade Blend or process chilli, vinegar and garlic until smooth. With motor operating, gradually add oil in a thin, steady stream until mixture thickens slightly.

preparation time *15 minutes (plus refrigeration time)*
cooking time *20 minutes* serves *4*
nutritional count per serving *33.4g total fat
(11.5g saturated fat); 2203kJ (527 cal);
39.8g carbohydrate; 10.4g protein; 6.0g fibre*

fennel, orange and red onion with quinoa

piri piri vegetables with polenta

mediterranean vegetables with oregano dressing

leeks and green onions with romesco sauce

mediterranean vegetables with oregano dressing

1 medium red capsicum (200g)
1 medium yellow capsicum (200g)
1 large red onion (300g), halved, cut into wedges
1 small kumara (250g), sliced thinly lengthways
2 baby eggplants (120g), sliced thinly lengthways
2 medium zucchini (240g), halved lengthways
340g jar artichoke hearts, drained, halved
100g seeded kalamata olives
1 small radicchio (150g), trimmed, leaves separated

oregano dressing
¼ cup (60ml) olive oil
2 tablespoons red wine vinegar
2 tablespoons lemon juice
2 cloves garlic, crushed
1 tablespoon finely chopped fresh oregano leaves

1 Make oregano dressing.

2 Quarter capsicums, discard seeds and membranes; cut capsicum into thick strips.

3 Cook capsicum on heated oiled barbecue until tender. Cook onion, kumara, eggplant, zucchini and artichoke, in batches, on heated oiled barbecue until tender.

4 Combine char-grilled vegetables, olives and dressing in large bowl; toss gently. Serve with radicchio.

oregano dressing Combine ingredients in screw-top jar; shake well.

preparation time *20 minutes*
cooking time *35 minutes* serves *4*
nutritional count per serving *14.8g total fat (2g saturated fat); 1104kJ (264 cal); 22.8g carbohydrate; 6.4g protein; 7.6g fibre*

This robust salad can be made ahead with great success: the flavours of the dressing's fresh oregano and lemon will permeate the grilled vegetables.

leeks and green onions with romesco sauce

16 pencil leeks (1.3kg), trimmed
30g butter, melted
1 tablespoon olive oil
300g green onions, trimmed

romesco sauce
1 teaspoon dried chilli flakes
¼ cup (60ml) extra virgin olive oil
1 large red capsicum (350g), chopped coarsely
2 cloves garlic, crushed
1 tablespoon slivered almonds, roasted
2 medium tomatoes (380g), chopped coarsely
1 tablespoon red wine vinegar

1 Make romesco sauce.

2 Wash leeks to remove any grit between leaves. Cook leeks on heated oiled barbecue, brushing with combined butter and oil, about 10 minutes or until browned and tender. Add onions; cook until tender.

3 Serve with romesco sauce.

romesco sauce Soak chilli flakes in 2 tablespoons hot water for 5 minutes; drain. Heat 1 tablespoon of the oil in medium frying pan; cook capsicum and garlic until soft but not coloured. Blend or process chilli with capsicum mixture, nuts and tomato until smooth. While motor is operating, gradually add rest of oil and vinegar; process until smooth.

preparation time *15 minutes*
cooking *15 minutes* serves *8*
nutritional count per serving *13.7g total fat (3.4g saturated fat); 748kJ (179 cal); 8.1g carbohydrate; 4.1g protein; 5g fibre*

zucchini with pumpkin and couscous

½ cup (100g) couscous
½ cup (125ml) boiling water
2 tablespoons lemon juice
2 teaspoons olive oil
¼ cup (40g) pine nuts
1 clove garlic, crushed
½ small red onion (50g), chopped finely
1 teaspoon smoked paprika
½ teaspoon ground cumin
½ teaspoon cayenne pepper
½ small red capsicum (75g), chopped finely
200g piece pumpkin, chopped finely
2 tablespoons finely chopped fresh flat-leaf parsley
6 medium zucchini (720g), halved lengthways

preserved lemon yogurt
½ cup (140g) greek-style yogurt
2 tablespoons finely chopped preserved lemon
2 tablespoons water

1 Make preserved lemon yogurt.

2 Combine couscous with the water and juice in large heatproof bowl, cover; stand about 5 minutes or until liquid is absorbed, fluffing with fork occasionally.

3 Heat oil in large saucepan; cook nuts, stirring, until browned lightly. Add garlic, onion and spices; cook, stirring, until onion softens. Add capsicum and pumpkin; cook, stirring, until pumpkin is just tender. Stir in couscous and parsley.

4 Meanwhile, cook zucchini on heated oiled barbecue until just tender.

5 Serve zucchini topped with couscous and drizzled with yogurt.

preserved lemon yogurt Combine ingredients in small bowl.

preparation time *20 minutes*
cooking time *20 minutes* serves *4*
nutritional count per serving *12.7g total fat (2.5g saturated fat); 1200kJ (287 cal); 30.1g carbohydrate; 10.1g protein; 4.9g fibre*

Preserved lemon is a North African specialty; lemons are quartered and preserved in salt and lemon juice. To use, remove and discard pulp, squeeze juice from rind, rinse well; slice rind thinly. Sold in jars or singly by delicatessens; store under refrigeration once opened.

sweet chilli corn with herb and lime butter

capsicum, fennel and onion salad

sweet chilli corn with herb and lime butter

8 corn cobs in husks (3.5kg)
2 cups (500ml) milk
⅔ cup (160ml) sweet chilli sauce

herb and lime butter
125g butter, softened
2 teaspoons finely grated lime rind
2 teaspoons lime juice
1 tablespoon coarsely chopped fresh coriander

1 Gently peel husks down each corn cob, keeping husks attached at the base. Remove as much silk as possible then bring husks back over corn cobs to enclose completely.

2 Place corn cobs in large bowl; add milk and enough cold water to completely submerge corn. Cover; refrigerate 3 hours or overnight.

3 Make herb and lime butter.

4 Drain corn, peel back husks; spread equal amounts of chilli sauce over each cob then bring husks back over cobs to enclose completely. Do not allow husks to dry out; cook as soon as possible after draining.

5 Cook corn on heated oiled barbecue about 25 minutes or until tender, turning occasionally. Serve with herb and lime butter.

herb and lime butter Combine ingredients in small bowl; spoon mixture onto piece of plastic wrap; enclose in plastic wrap. Shape into log; refrigerate until firm.

preparation time *20 minutes (plus refrigeration time)*
cooking time *20 minutes* serves 8
nutritional count per serving *18.6g total fat (10.4g saturated fat); 1647kJ (394 cal); 44.7g carbohydrate; 12g protein; 11.3g fibre*

Freeze leftover butter to use on steak or bread.

capsicum, fennel and onion salad

2 baby fennel bulbs (260g), trimmed, quartered
1 small yellow capsicum (150g), sliced thickly
1 small red capsicum (150g), sliced thickly
2 small red onions (200g), cut into wedges
2 tablespoons olive oil
1 clove garlic, crushed

balsamic dressing
1 tablespoon lemon juice
2 tablespoons olive oil
1 tablespoon balsamic vinegar
1 clove garlic, crushed
1 tablespoon finely chopped fresh oregano

1 Make balsamic dressing.

2 Combine vegetables with oil and garlic; stand 30 minutes.

3 Cook vegetables on heated oiled barbecue until browned and cooked through.

4 Serve vegetables, warm or cold, drizzled with balsamic dressing.

balsamic dressing Combine ingredients in screw-top jar; shake well.

preparation time *15 minutes (plus standing time)*
cooking time *20 minutes* serves 4
nutritional count per serving *18.4g total fat (2.6g saturated fat); 849kJ (203 cal); 6.5g carbohydrate; 2.3g protein; 2.6g fibre*

Recipe can be prepared several hours ahead.

beef & veal

chilli-rubbed hickory-smoked rib-eye steaks, page 200

Veal has a low fat content and can easily dry out; cook over a low heat, away from the direct flame of the barbecue. For medium-rare beef, cook directly over the flame, and for well-done, seal the surface over high heat then move to a less intense part of the barbecue to finish cooking.

chilli-rubbed hickory-smoked rib-eye steaks

1 tablespoon finely grated lemon rind
2 teaspoons chilli powder
2 teaspoons dried thyme
1 teaspoon smoked paprika
2 tablespoons olive oil
2 cloves garlic, crushed
4 x 200g beef rib-eye steaks
100g hickory smoking chips
2 cups (500ml) water

1 Combine rind, chilli, thyme, paprika, oil and garlic in large bowl; add beef, turn to coat in mixture. Cover; refrigerate 3 hours or overnight.

2 Soak chips in the water in medium bowl; stand 3 hours or overnight.

3 Place drained chips in smoke box alongside beef on grill plate. Cook beef in covered barbecue, using indirect heat, following manufacturer's directions, about 10 minutes or until cooked as desired.

preparation time *10 minutes (plus refrigeration time)*
cooking time *10 minutes* serves *4*
nutritional count per serving *27.3g total fat (8.9g saturated fat); 1726kJ (413 cal); 0.4g carbohydrate; 41.1g protein; 0.7g fibre*

You need smoking chips and a smoke box for this recipe. The smoke box and hickory smoking chips are available at most barbecue supply stores, as are other varieties of wood chips that can also be used to smoke meat on the barbecue.

cheese-stuffed steaks with radicchio salad

80g brie cheese
4 x 125g beef eye-fillet steaks
1 small radicchio (150g), trimmed, quartered
1 cup (120g) roasted pecans, chopped coarsely
1 large pear (330g), unpeeled, cored, sliced thickly
1 cup loosely packed fresh flat-leaf parsley leaves
¼ cup (60ml) olive oil
2 tablespoons lemon juice

1 Slice cheese thickly into four pieces. Slice steaks in half horizontally. Sandwich cheese slices between steak halves; tie with kitchen string to secure.

2 Cook beef on heated oiled barbecue until cooked as desired.

3 Meanwhile, cook radicchio on heated oiled barbecue until browned lightly. Combine radicchio with remaining ingredients in medium bowl; serve with beef.

preparation time *20 minutes*
cooking time *20 minutes* serves *4*
nutritional count per serving *48.1g total fat (9.8g saturated fat); 2596kJ (621 cal); 12g carbohydrate; 34.2g protein; 5.4g fibre*

We used a triple-cream brie cheese here; you can replace it with the more easily found blue-vein variety, if you prefer, but choose one that's mild and very creamy.

cheese-stuffed steaks with radicchio salad

steak and vegetables with baba ghanoush

3 cloves garlic, crushed
2 tablespoons olive oil
2 teaspoons finely grated lemon rind
2 medium red capsicums (400g), sliced thickly
2 large zucchini (300g), halved widthways then
   sliced thinly lengthways
4 x 150g beef eye-fillet steaks
½ cup (120g) baba ghanoush
⅓ cup loosely packed fresh mint leaves

1 Combine garlic, oil, rind, capsicum, zucchini and beef in large bowl. Cook beef and vegetables on heated oiled barbecue until beef is cooked as desired and vegetables are tender.

2 Divide vegetables among serving plates; top with beef. Serve with baba ghanoush and mint.

preparation time *15 minutes*
cooking time *20 minutes* serves *4*
nutritional count per serving *17.3g total fat*
(4.6g saturated fat); 1354kJ (324 cal);
5.9g carbohydrate; 34.2g protein; 3.6g fibre

spicy beef and bean salad

¼ cup (60ml) olive oil
35g packet taco seasoning mix
600g piece beef eye fillet
2 tablespoons lime juice
1 clove garlic, crushed
420g can four-bean mix, rinsed, drained
310g can corn kernels, rinsed, drained
2 lebanese cucumbers (260g), chopped finely
1 small red onion (100g), chopped finely
1 large red capsicum (350g), chopped finely
½ cup coarsely chopped fresh coriander
1 fresh long red chilli, chopped finely

1 Combine 1 tablespoon of the oil with the seasoning and beef in medium bowl. Cook beef on heated oiled barbecue until cooked as desired. Cover beef; stand 5 minutes then slice thinly.

2 Meanwhile, whisk remaining oil, juice and garlic in large bowl. Add remaining ingredients; toss gently to combine. Serve beef with salad; sprinkle with coriander leaves, if desired.

preparation time *10 minutes*
cooking time *20 minutes* serves *4*
nutritional count per serving *22.2g total fat*
(5.2g saturated fat); 2111kJ (505 cal);
30.9g carbohydrate; 40.4g protein; 9.3g fibre

steak and vegetables with baba ghanoush

spicy beef and bean salad

scotch fillet with white bean and spinach salad

beef teriyaki platter

scotch fillet with white bean and spinach salad

4 x 200g beef scotch fillet steaks
1 clove garlic, crushed
2cm piece fresh ginger (10g), grated
⅓ cup (80ml) lime juice
2 teaspoons sesame oil
¼ cup loosely packed fresh mint leaves
2 x 420g cans white beans, rinsed, drained
100g baby spinach leaves
1 small red onion (100g), sliced thinly

chilli jam
2 medium tomatoes (300g), chopped coarsely
2 tablespoons water
1 tablespoon brown sugar
¼ cup (60ml) sweet chilli sauce
1 fresh long red chilli, chopped finely
2 tablespoons coarsely chopped fresh coriander

1   Make chilli jam.

2   Cook beef on heated oiled barbecue until cooked as desired. Cover beef; stand 5 minutes.

3   Meanwhile, combine garlic, ginger, juice and oil in screw-top jar; shake well.

4   Combine mint, beans, spinach, onion and dressing in large bowl.

5   Serve beef with white bean and spinach salad; accompany with chilli jam.

chilli jam Combine tomato, the water, sugar, sauce and chilli in medium saucepan; bring to the boil. Reduce heat; simmer, uncovered, about 20 minutes or until jam thickens. Remove from heat; cool 5 minutes. Stir in coriander.

preparation time *20 minutes*
cooking time *55 minutes* serves *4*
nutritional count per serving *15.4g total fat
(5.5g saturated fat); 1648kJ (394 cal);
13.3g carbohydrate; 47.6g protein; 6.1g fibre*

beef teriyaki platter

⅓ cup (80ml) teriyaki sauce
3cm piece fresh ginger (15g), grated
1 clove garlic, crushed
3 thick beef sirloin steaks (600g), trimmed
500g thick asparagus, trimmed
8 green onions, trimmed
1 teaspoon wasabi paste
¼ cup (60ml) japanese soy sauce

1   Combine teriyaki sauce, ginger and garlic in large bowl; add beef, turn to coat in marinade. Cover, refrigerate 3 hours or overnight.

2   Drain beef; discard marinade. Cook beef on heated oiled barbecue until cooked as desired. Cover beef; stand 5 minutes then slice thinly.

3   Meanwhile, cook asparagus and onions on heated oiled barbecue until just tender.

4   Serve beef with asparagus and onions; accompany with wasabi, soy sauce, and steamed rice, if desired.

preparation time *20 minutes (plus refrigeration time)*
cooking time *10 minutes* serves *4*
nutritional count per serving *9.3g total fat
(3.8g saturated fat); 1032kJ (247 cal);
3.4g carbohydrate; 36.1g protein; 2g fibre*

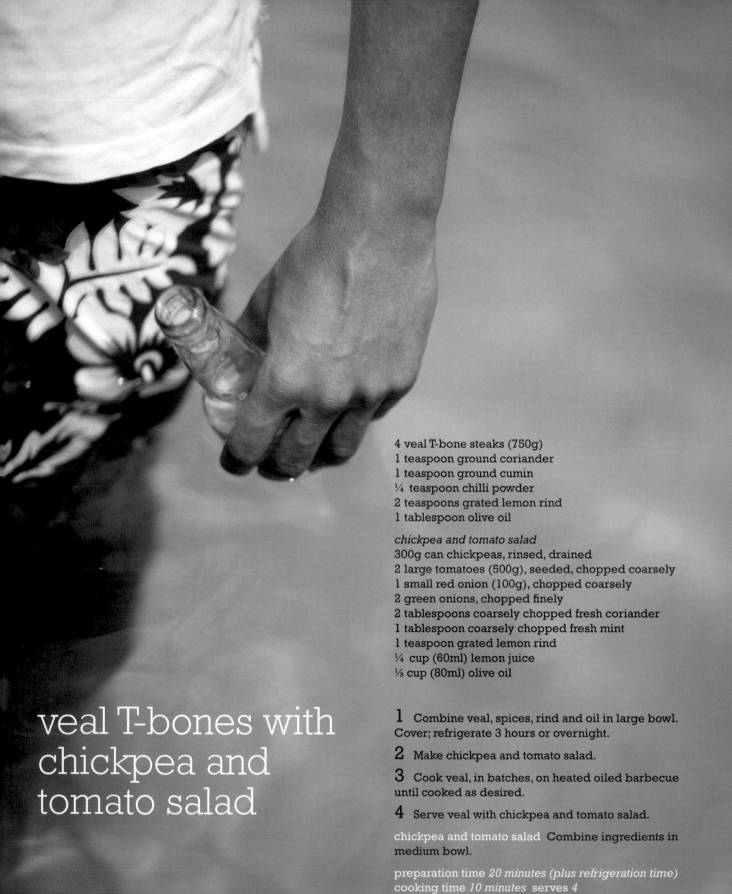

4 veal T-bone steaks (750g)
1 teaspoon ground coriander
1 teaspoon ground cumin
¼ teaspoon chilli powder
2 teaspoons grated lemon rind
1 tablespoon olive oil

chickpea and tomato salad
300g can chickpeas, rinsed, drained
2 large tomatoes (500g), seeded, chopped coarsely
1 small red onion (100g), chopped coarsely
2 green onions, chopped finely
2 tablespoons coarsely chopped fresh coriander
1 tablespoon coarsely chopped fresh mint
1 teaspoon grated lemon rind
¼ cup (60ml) lemon juice
⅓ cup (80ml) olive oil

veal T-bones with chickpea and tomato salad

1 Combine veal, spices, rind and oil in large bowl. Cover; refrigerate 3 hours or overnight.

2 Make chickpea and tomato salad.

3 Cook veal, in batches, on heated oiled barbecue until cooked as desired.

4 Serve veal with chickpea and tomato salad.

chickpea and tomato salad Combine ingredients in medium bowl.

preparation time *20 minutes (plus refrigeration time)*
cooking time *10 minutes* serves *4*
nutritional count per serving *26.7g total fat
(4.2g saturated fat); 1760kJ (421 cal);
11.4g carbohydrate; 32g protein; 4.4g fibre*

port-smoked beef

chilli and honey barbecued steak

port-smoked beef

2 tablespoons olive oil
2 cloves garlic, crushed
¼ cup (60ml) port
2 tablespoons coarsely chopped fresh oregano
1.5kg beef fillet
handful smoking chips
1 cup (250ml) port, extra

1 Combine oil, garlic, port and oregano in large bowl; add beef, turn to coat in marinade. Cover; refrigerate 3 hours or overnight.

2 Combine smoking chips and extra port in small bowl. Cover; stand 3 hours or overnight.

3 Cook beef, uncovered, on heated oiled barbecue until just browned all over. Place beef in lightly oiled disposable baking dish. Place drained smoking chips in smoke box; place beside beef on barbecue.

4 Cook beef in covered barbecue, using indirect heat, following manufacturer's instructions, about 1½ hours or until cooked as desired.

preparation time *10 minutes (plus refrigeration time)*
cooking time *1 hour 35 minutes* serves *8*
nutritional count per serving *15.8g total fat (5.3g saturated fat); 1505kJ (360 cal); 5.1g carbohydrate; 39g protein; 0.1g fibre*

You need smoking chips and a smoke box for this recipe; they are available from barbecue supply stores.

chilli and honey barbecued steak

2 tablespoons barbecue sauce
1 tablespoon worcestershire sauce
1 tablespoon honey
1 fresh long red chilli, chopped finely
1 clove garlic, crushed
4 x 200g new-york cut steaks

coleslaw
2 tablespoons mayonnaise
1 tablespoon white wine vinegar
2 cups finely shredded white cabbage
1 cup finely shredded red cabbage
1 medium carrot (120g), grated coarsely
3 green onions, sliced thinly

1 Combine sauces, honey, chilli and garlic in large bowl; add beef, turn to coat in mixture.

2 Cook beef on heated oiled barbecue until cooked as desired.

3 Meanwhile, make coleslaw. Serve beef with coleslaw.

coleslaw Place mayonnaise and vinegar in screw-top jar; shake well. Combine dressing in large bowl with cabbages, carrot and onions; toss gently.

preparation time *25 minutes*
cooking time *10 minutes* serves *4*
nutritional count per serving *15.2g total fat (5.4g saturated fat); 1605kJ (384 cal); 16.6g carbohydrate; 44g protein; 3.6g fibre*

mexican-spiced beef with chilli beans

2 cups (400g) dried black beans
2 pasilla chillies (10g)
¼ cup (60ml) boiling water
2 tablespoons olive oil
1 medium brown onion (150g), chopped finely
3 cloves garlic, crushed
¼ cup (70g) tomato paste
4 medium tomatoes (600g), chopped coarsely
½ cup (125ml) water
2 tablespoons lime juice
2 tablespoons brown sugar
1 tablespoon dried marjoram
2 teaspoons smoked paprika
1kg beef rump steak
8 large flour tortillas (320g)
1 small iceberg lettuce, trimmed, shredded finely
⅔ cup (160g) sour cream
1 small red onion (100g), sliced thinly
⅓ cup firmly packed fresh coriander leaves

1 Place beans in large bowl, cover with water; stand overnight. Rinse under cold water; drain. Cook beans in large saucepan of boiling water, uncovered, until tender; drain. Rinse under cold water; drain.

2 Meanwhile, soak chillies in the boiling water in a small heatproof bowl 20 minutes; blend or process chillies and soaking water until smooth.

3 Heat half the oil in large saucepan; cook brown onion and garlic, stirring, until onion softens. Add chilli mixture, paste, tomato, the water, juice and sugar; bring to the boil. Remove from heat; blend or process until smooth.

4 Return chilli mixture to pan, add beans; simmer, covered, 20 minutes. Uncover; simmer about 10 minutes or until sauce thickens.

5 Meanwhile, combine marjoram, paprika and remaining oil in large bowl; add beef, turn to coat in mixture. Cook beef, both sides, on heated oiled barbecue until cooked as desired. Cover beef; stand 10 minutes then slice thinly.

6 Divide tortillas into two batches; wrap each batch in a double thickness of foil. Heat tortilla parcels, turning occasionally, on barbecue about 5 minutes or until warm. Serve tortillas with chilli beans, beef, lettuce, sour cream, red onion and coriander.

preparation time *25 minutes (plus standing time)*
cooking time *1 hour 20 minutes* serves *4*
nutritional count per serving *49.8g total fat (20.4g saturated fat); 5158kJ (1234 cal); 96.2g carbohydrate; 92g protein; 21.4g fibre*

T-bones with potato pancakes

3 fresh long red chillies, chopped finely
2cm piece fresh ginger (10g), grated
2 cloves garlic, crushed
2 tablespoons olive oil
4 x 300g beef T-bone steaks
4 trimmed corn cobs (1kg)
4 medium potatoes (800g), grated coarsely
50g butter

1 Combine chilli, ginger, garlic and oil in large bowl; add beef, turn to coat in mixture. Cook beef on heated oiled barbecue until cooked as desired. Cover beef; stand 5 minutes.

2 Meanwhile, cook corn, turning occasionally, on heated oiled barbecue until tender.

3 To make potato pancakes, squeeze excess moisture from potato; divide into four portions. Heat half the butter on heated barbecue; cook potato portions, flattening with spatula, until browned both sides.

4 Spread corn with remaining butter; serve with beef and potato pancakes.

preparation time *20 minutes*
cooking time *30 minutes* serves *4*
nutritional count per serving *33.1g total fat (13g saturated fat); 3118kJ (746 cal); 53.4g carbohydrate; 52.8g protein; 11.4g fibre*

mustard-crumbed beef fillet with rocket salad

¼ cup (70g) prepared horseradish
1 tablespoon olive oil
1kg piece beef eye fillet
2 tablespoons wholegrain mustard
1 tablespoon coarsely chopped fresh flat-leaf parsley
½ cup (35g) fresh breadcrumbs
1 tablespoon butter, melted

rocket salad
100g baby rocket leaves
1 medium red onion (170g), sliced thinly
8 green onions, sliced thinly
¼ cup (40g) roasted pine nuts
⅓ cup (80ml) balsamic vinegar
⅓ cup (80ml) olive oil

1 Combine horseradish and oil in large bowl; add beef, turn to coat in mixture. Cover; refrigerate 3 hours or overnight.

2 Cook beef, uncovered, on heated oiled barbecue turning, until browned all over; remove from barbecue.

3 Combine mustard, parsley and breadcrumbs in small bowl with half the butter. Brush beef with remaining butter; press breadcrumb mixture over top of beef.

4 Cook beef in covered barbecue, using indirect heat, following manufacturer's instructions, about 40 minutes or until crust is browned and beef is cooked as desired. Cover beef; stand 10 minutes then slice thickly.

5 Meanwhile, make rocket salad.

6 Serve beef with rocket salad.

rocket salad Combine ingredients in large bowl.

preparation time *20 minutes (plus refrigeration time)*
cooking time *50 minutes* serves *6*
nutritional count per serving *34.2g total fat (9.1g saturated fat); 2082kJ (498 cal); 8.7g carbohydrate; 38.4g protein; 1.9g fibre*

T-bones with potato pancakes

mustard-crumbed beef fillet with rocket salad

za'atar-spiced veal loin chops with fattoush

4 x 200g veal loin chops

za'atar
1 tablespoon sumac
1 tablespoon toasted sesame seeds
2 teaspoons finely chopped fresh thyme
1 tablespoon olive oil
1 teaspoon dried marjoram

fattoush
2 large pitta breads (160g)
4 medium tomatoes (600g), cut into wedges
2 lebanese cucumbers (260g), seeded, sliced thinly
1 medium green capsicum (200g), cut into 2cm pieces
3 green onions, sliced thinly
1 cup coarsely chopped fresh flat-leaf parsley
½ cup coarsely chopped fresh mint
½ cup (125ml) olive oil
¼ cup (60ml) lemon juice
2 cloves garlic, crushed

1 Make za'atar. Make fattoush.

2 Cook veal on heated oiled barbecue until cooked as desired. Sprinkle a tablespoon of the za'atar equally over the veal; serve with fattoush.

za'atar Combine ingredients in small bowl.

fattoush Cook bread on heated oiled barbecue until crisp; break into small pieces. Combine tomato, cucumber, capsicum, onion and herbs in large bowl. Just before serving, toss bread and combined oil, juice and garlic into salad.

preparation time *15 minutes*
cooking time *20 minutes* serves *4*
nutritional count per serving *38.9g total fat*
(5.9g saturated fat); 2587kJ (619 cal);
27.8g carbohydrate; 36.5g protein; 17.1g fibre

veal cutlets with green olive salsa

2 tablespoons olive oil
2 cloves garlic, crushed
1 tablespoon finely chopped fresh oregano
2 teaspoons finely grated lemon rind
1 tablespoon lemon juice
4 x 150g veal cutlets

green olive salsa
1 tablespoon lemon juice
¼ cup coarsely chopped fresh flat-leaf parsley
½ cup (80g) finely chopped large green olives
1 small green capsicum (150g), chopped finely
1 tablespoon olive oil
1 clove garlic, crushed
1 tablespoon finely chopped fresh oregano

barbecued kipflers
1.5kg kipfler potatoes, unpeeled
¼ cup fresh thyme leaves
1 tablespoon coarsely grated lemon rind
2 cloves garlic, crushed
⅓ cup (80ml) olive oil
¼ cup (60ml) lemon

1 Make green olive salsa. Make barbecued kipflers.

2 Meanwhile, combine oil, garlic, oregano, rind and juice in small bowl; brush mixture over veal. Cook veal on heated oiled barbecue until cooked as desired.

3 Serve veal with salsa and barbecued kipflers.

green olive salsa Combine ingredients in small bowl.

barbecued kipflers Boil, steam or microwave potatoes until tender; drain. Halve potatoes lengthways. Combine thyme, rind, garlic, oil, juice and potato in large bowl; toss to coat potato in mixture. Cook potato on heated oiled barbecue about 15 minutes or until browned lightly.

preparation time 20 minutes
cooking time 45 minutes serves 4
nutritional count per serving 35g total fat
(5.3g saturated fat); 2897kJ (692 cal);
55.9g carbohydrate; 32.6g protein; 9.1g fibre

caramelised onion with calves liver and potatoes

5 small red onions (500g), sliced thinly
1 tablespoon brown sugar
1½ tablespoons balsamic vinegar
3 medium potatoes (600g), unpeeled,
    cut into 1cm slices
1 tablespoon olive oil
600g calves liver, sliced thinly

1 Cook onion on heated oiled barbecue flat plate until browned lightly. Sprinkle onion with sugar and vinegar; cook, turning constantly, until onion is caramelised. Transfer onion to small bowl; cover to keep warm.

2 Meanwhile, boil, steam or microwave potato until tender, drain; combine in large bowl with oil. Cook potato on heated oiled barbecue until browned lightly.

3 Meanwhile, cook liver on heated oiled barbecue until browned both sides and just cooked through. Serve liver with onion and potato.

preparation time 15 minutes
cooking time 30 minutes serves 4
nutritional count per serving 13.1g total fat
(3.3g saturated fat); 1660kJ (397 cal);
34.2g carbohydrate; 33g protein; 4g fibre

veal cutlets with green olive salsa

caramelised onion with calves liver and potatoes

barbecued scotch fillet

fennel veal chops with garlic mustard butter

barbecued scotch fillet

¼ cup (60ml) barbecue sauce
2 tablespoons american mustard
4 cloves garlic, crushed
½ cup (125ml) beer
1.5kg piece beef scotch fillet

1 Combine sauce, mustard, garlic and beer in large bowl; add beef, turn to coat in mixture. Cover; refrigerate 3 hours or overnight.

2 Place beef and marinade in oiled disposable baking dish. Cook in covered barbecue, using indirect heat, following manufacturer's instructions about 1½ hours or until cooked as desired. Cover beef; stand 15 minutes then slice thinly.

preparation time *10 minutes*
(plus refrigeration and standing time)
cooking time *1 hour 30 minutes* serves *6*
nutritional count per serving *14.2g total fat
(5.9g saturated fat); 1488kJ (356 cal);
5.9g carbohydrate; 49.7g protein; 0.6g fibre*

fennel veal chops with garlic mustard butter

2 teaspoons fennel seeds
1 teaspoon sea salt
½ teaspoon cracked black pepper
2 tablespoons olive oil
4 x 200g veal chops
4 flat mushrooms (320g)
80g butter, softened
1 tablespoon coarsely chopped fresh flat-leaf parsley
1 clove garlic, crushed
1 tablespoon wholegrain mustard
80g baby rocket leaves

1 Using mortar and pestle, coarsely crush combined seeds, salt and pepper; stir in oil. Rub mixture over veal.

2 Cook veal and mushrooms on heated oiled barbecue until browned both sides and cooked as desired.

3 Meanwhile, combine butter, parsley, garlic and mustard in small bowl.

4 Divide rocket among serving plates; top each with mushroom, veal then butter mixture.

preparation time *10 minutes*
cooking time *15 minutes* serves *4*
nutritional count per serving *29.7g total fat
(13.2g saturated fat); 1831kJ (438 cal);
2.1g carbohydrate; 39.9g protein; 2.7g fibre*

cantonese beef patties with gai lan

800g beef mince
1 medium brown onion (150g), chopped finely
2cm piece fresh ginger (10g), grated
1 fresh small red thai chilli, chopped finely
227g can water chestnuts, rinsed, drained, chopped finely
¼ cup finely chopped fresh chives
1 egg
½ cup (35g) fresh breadcrumbs
1 tablespoon hoisin sauce
3 cloves garlic, crushed
1 tablespoon water
2 tablespoons oyster sauce
⅓ cup (80ml) hoisin sauce, extra
2 teaspoons sesame oil
1kg gai lan, chopped coarsely

1 Combine beef, onion, ginger, chilli, chestnuts, chives, egg, breadcrumbs, hoisin sauce and two-thirds of the garlic in large bowl; shape mixture into eight patties.

2 Combine the water, oyster sauce, extra hoisin sauce and remaining garlic in small bowl. Reserve ¼ cup hoisin mixture.

3 Brush patties with remaining hoisin mixture; cook patties on heated oiled barbecue until browned both sides and cooked through.

4 Heat sesame oil on barbecue plate; cook gai lan until wilted. Serve gai lan topped with patties; drizzle with reserved hoisin mixture.

preparation time *30 minutes*
cooking time *15 minutes* serves *4*
nutritional count per serving *20.2g total fat (6.8g saturated fat); 2077kJ (497 cal); 26.6g carbohydrate; 48g protein; 8.3g fibre*

Hoisin is a sweet, thick chinese barbecue sauce made from salted fermented soya beans, onion and garlic. It is available from Asian food shops and most supermarkets.

scotch fillet steaks with onion and garlic mushrooms

½ cup (125ml) dry red wine
2 tablespoons coarsely chopped fresh basil
2 cloves garlic, crushed
6 x 200g beef scotch fillet steaks
20g butter
6 medium red onions (1kg), sliced thinly
⅓ cup (75g) firmly packed brown sugar
¼ cup (60ml) red wine vinegar
6 large flat mushrooms (840g)
2 tablespoons olive oil
1 clove garlic, crushed, extra
1 teaspoon lemon pepper

1 Combine wine, basil and garlic in large bowl; add beef, turn to coat in mixture. Cover; refrigerate 3 hours or overnight.

2 Melt butter in large frying pan; cook onion, stirring, until soft and browned lightly. Stir in sugar and vinegar; cook, stirring constantly, about 20 minutes or until onion is well browned and mixture has thickened.

3 Brush mushrooms with combined oil, extra garlic and lemon pepper; cook on heated oiled barbecue until tender.

4 Drain beef; discard marinade. Cook beef on heated oiled barbecue until cooked as desired.

5 Top each piece of beef with a mushroom and a little caramelised onion.

preparation time *30 minutes (plus refrigeration time)*
cooking time *45 minutes* serves *6*
nutritional count per serving *21g total fat*
(7.7g saturated fat); 1977kJ (473 cal);
21.4g carbohydrate; 44.8g protein; 2.5g fibre

veal chops with fennel and mandarin

4 x 200g veal chops
2 baby fennel bulbs (260g), trimmed,
   halved lengthways
4 small mandarins (400g), peeled,
   halved horizontally

salsa verde
¼ cup finely chopped fresh flat-leaf parsley
¼ cup finely chopped fresh mint
1 tablespoon finely chopped fennel tips
¼ cup finely chopped fresh chives
1 tablespoon wholegrain mustard
2 tablespoons lemon juice
2 tablespoons rinsed, drained baby capers,
   chopped finely
1 clove garlic, crushed
⅓ cup (80ml) olive oil

1 Cook veal on heated oiled barbecue until cooked as desired.

2 Cook fennel and mandarin on heated oiled barbecue until just browned.

3 Make salsa verde.

4 Serve veal, fennel and mandarin topped with salsa verde.

salsa verde Combine ingredients in small bowl.

preparation time *25 minutes*
cooking time *20 minutes* serves *4*
nutritional count per serving *21.6g total fat
(3.5g saturated fat); 1492kJ (357 cal);
8.4g carbohydrate; 30.4g protein; 3.3g fibre*

beef burger with eggplant and rocket

⅓ cup (95g) yogurt
⅓ cup (80g) hummus
1 medium eggplant (300g)
500g beef mince
2 cloves garlic, crushed
1 tablespoon tomato paste
1 small brown onion (80g), chopped finely
1 fresh small red thai chilli, chopped finely
½ cup coarsely chopped fresh basil
½ cup (35g) stale breadcrumbs
1 egg
1 loaf turkish bread (430g), cut into quarters
40g baby rocket leaves

1 Combine yogurt and hummus in small bowl.

2 Cut eggplant into 6 slices lengthways; discard two skin-side pieces.

3 Combine beef, garlic, paste, onion, chilli, basil, breadcrumbs and egg in large bowl; shape mixture into four patties. Cook patties and eggplant, in batches, on heated oiled barbecue until browned both sides and cooked through.

4 Halve bread pieces horizontally; toast bread on heated oiled barbecue. Spread cut-sides with yogurt mixture; sandwich rocket, eggplant and patties between toast pieces.

preparation time *20 minutes*
cooking time *15 minutes* serves *4*
nutritional count per serving *19.3g total fat
(6.4g saturated fat); 2546kJ (609 cal);
61.8g carbohydrate; 42.6g protein; 7.5g fibre*

veal chops with fennel and mandarin

beef burger with eggplant and rocket

veal with salsa verde and potato rösti

steak sandwich with capsicum and ricotta

veal with salsa verde and potato rösti

800g piece veal tenderloin, halved lengthways
4 medium potatoes (800g)
1 egg

salsa verde
⅔ cup finely chopped fresh flat-leaf parsley
⅓ cup finely chopped fresh mint
⅓ cup finely chopped fresh dill
⅓ cup finely chopped fresh chives
1 tablespoon wholegrain mustard
¼ cup (60ml) lemon juice
¼ cup (50g) rinsed, drained baby capers
2 cloves garlic, crushed
½ cup (125ml) olive oil

1 Make salsa verde.

2 Rub veal with half the salsa verde; cook veal on heated oiled barbecue until cooked as desired. Cover veal; stand 5 minutes then slice thickly.

3 Meanwhile, grate potatoes coarsely. Squeeze excess moisture from potato. Combine potato and egg in medium bowl; divide into eight equal portions. Cook portions on heated oiled flat plate, flattening with spatula, until rösti are browned both sides. Drain on absorbent paper.

4 Serve veal with rösti and remaining salsa verde.

salsa verde Combine ingredients in medium bowl.

preparation time *20 minutes*
cooking time *15 minutes* serves *4*
nutritional count per serving *33.2g total fat
(5.2g saturated fat); 2537kJ (607 cal);
24.3g carbohydrate; 51.1g protein; 4g fibre*

steak sandwich with capsicum and ricotta

2 medium red capsicums (400g)
¾ cup (180g) ricotta cheese
2 tablespoons coarsely chopped fresh chervil
2 teaspoons lemon juice
4 x 125g beef minute steaks
1 tablespoon cracked black pepper
4 slices rye sourdough bread (180g)
1 tablespoon olive oil
2 cloves garlic, crushed
40g baby rocket leaves

1 Quarter capsicums; discard seeds and membranes. Cook capsicum on heated oiled barbecue, skin-side down, until skin blisters and blackens. Cover capsicum pieces in plastic or paper 5 minutes then peel away skin.

2 Meanwhile, combine cheese, chervil and juice in small bowl.

3 Sprinkle beef, both sides, with pepper; cook on heated oiled barbecue until cooked as desired.

4 Brush one side of each bread slice with combined oil and garlic; toast bread on heated oiled barbecue. Spread toast slices with cheese mixture; top with capsicum, beef then rocket.

preparation time *15 minutes*
cooking time *15 minutes* serves *4*
nutritional count per serving *19.3g total fat
(7.6g saturated fat); 1793kJ (429cal);
25g carbohydrate; 36.8g protein; 3.9g fibre*

veal with tomato and caper salsa

6 baby eggplants (360g), halved lengthways
6 small zucchini (540g), halved lengthways
2 tablespoons olive oil
12 veal cutlets (2kg)
1 tablespoon cracked black pepper
1 tablespoon small fresh basil leaves

tomato and caper salsa
2 medium tomatoes (300g), seeded, chopped finely
1 small red onion (100g), chopped finely
1 clove garlic, crushed
2 tablespoons rinsed, drained baby capers
1 tablespoon balsamic vinegar
1 tablespoon olive oil

1 Cook eggplant and zucchini, in batches, on heated oiled barbecue until browned and tender, brushing with the oil. Cover to keep warm.

2 Sprinkle veal with pepper; cook on heated oiled barbecue until cooked as desired.

3 Meanwhile, make tomato and caper salsa.

4 Serve veal with eggplant, zucchini and salsa; sprinkle with basil.

tomato and caper salsa Combine tomato, onion, garlic, capers, vinegar and oil in small bowl.

preparation time *15 minutes*
cooking time *20 minutes* serves *6*
nutritional count per serving *15.7g total fat (3.2g saturated fat); 1722kJ (412 cal); 4.5g carbohydrate; 62.3g protein; 3.4g fibre*

veal cutlets with onion marmalade

2 teaspoons olive oil
1 clove garlic, crushed
1 teaspoon cracked black pepper
4 x 150g veal cutlets
2 corn cobs (800g), trimmed, cut into 3cm pieces
500g asparagus, trimmed

onion marmalade
20g butter
2 large red onions (600g), sliced thinly
⅓ cup (75g) firmly packed brown sugar
¼ cup (60ml) cider vinegar
2 tablespoons orange juice
2 teaspoons finely chopped fresh rosemary

1 Combine oil, garlic and pepper in large bowl; add veal, toss to coat in marinade. Cover; refrigerate until required.

2 Meanwhile, make onion marmalade.

3 Cook corn and asparagus on heated oiled barbecue until browned lightly and tender; cover to keep warm.

4 Cook veal on heated oiled barbecue until cooked as desired. Serve veal, corn and asparagus topped with onion marmalade.

onion marmalade Heat butter in medium frying pan; cook onion, stirring, until soft and browned lightly. Add sugar, vinegar and juice; cook, stirring, about 15 minutes or until onion caramelises. Remove from heat; stir in rosemary.

preparation time *15 minutes*
cooking time *40 minutes* serves *4*
nutritional information per serving *11.7g total fat (4.1g saturated fat) 1965kJ (470 cal) 50.8g carbohydrate 40.1g protein 10.4g fibre*

veal with tomato and caper salsa

veal cutlets with onion marmalade

You need 80g watercress to get the amount of trimmed watercress required for this recipe. You can use ciabatta, focaccia or even individual turkish breads (pide) for this recipe.

steak sandwich with tarragon and tomato salsa

4 x 125g beef scotch fillet steaks
2 cloves garlic, crushed
1 tablespoon dijon mustard
1 tablespoon olive oil
8 thick slices bread (320g)
⅓ cup (100g) mayonnaise
40g trimmed watercress

tarragon and tomato salsa
2 cloves garlic, crushed
3 large egg tomatoes (270g), quartered, sliced thinly
½ small red onion (50g), sliced thinly
1 tablespoon finely chopped fresh tarragon

1 Combine beef, garlic, mustard and half the oil in medium bowl.

2 Make tarragon and tomato salsa.

3 Cook beef on heated oiled barbecue until cooked as desired. Cover beef; stand 5 minutes.

4 Meanwhile, brush both sides of bread with remaining oil; toast on heated oiled barbecue. Spread one side of each slice with mayonnaise; sandwich watercress, beef and salsa between slices.

tarragon and tomato salsa Combine ingredients in medium bowl.

preparation time *15 minutes*
cooking time *15 minutes* serves *4*
nutritional count per serving *21.6g total fat (4.6g saturated fat); 2161kJ (517 cal); 43.3g carbohydrate; 35g protein; 4.2g fibre*

satay beef skewers

160ml can coconut cream
¼ cup (70g) crunchy peanut butter
1 clove garlic, crushed
1 fresh small red thai chilli, chopped finely
1 tablespoon fish sauce
1 tablespoon kecap manis
800g piece beef eye fillet, cut into 3cm cubes

1   Combine coconut cream, peanut butter, garlic, chilli, sauce and kecap manis in medium jug.

2   Thread beef onto 8 bamboo skewers. Brush ½ cup of the satay sauce over beef. Cook skewers on heated oiled barbecue until cooked as desired.

3   Bring remaining satay sauce to the boil in small saucepan; drizzle over skewers to serve.

preparation time *30 minutes*
cooking time *15 minutes* serves *4*
nutritional count per serving *29.2g total fat (13.8g saturated fat); 1986kJ (475 cal); 3.6g carbohydrate; 48.5g protein; 2.8g fibre*

You need 8 bamboo skewers for this recipe. Soak skewers in cold water for at least an hour before using to prevent them from splintering and scorching during cooking.

scotch fillet in barbecue sauce

2 tablespoons brown sugar
2 tablespoons barbecue sauce
2 tablespoons tomato sauce
2 teaspoons smoked paprika
1 tablespoon red wine vinegar
4 x 200g beef scotch fillet steaks

1   Combine sugar, sauces, paprika and vinegar in large bowl; add beef, turn to coat in mixture.

2   Cook beef on heated oiled barbecue until cooked as desired. Cover beef; stand 5 minutes before serving.

preparation time *5 minutes*
cooking time *10 minutes* serves *4*
nutritional count per serving *12g total fat (5g saturated fat); 1400kJ (335 cal); 13.8g carbohydrate; 42.4g protein; 0.3g fibre*

Either salad or barbecued vegetables will go well with the steak.

satay beef skewers

scotch fillet in barbecue sauce

fajitas with salsa cruda and avocado mash

2 tablespoons vegetable oil
⅓ cup (80ml) lime juice
¼ cup coarsely chopped fresh oregano
2 cloves garlic, crushed
¼ cup coarsely chopped fresh coriander
2 teaspoons ground cumin
800g beef skirt steak
1 medium red capsicum (200g), sliced thickly
1 medium green capsicum (200g), sliced thickly
1 medium yellow capsicum (200g), sliced thickly
1 large red onion (300g), sliced thickly
20 small flour tortillas

salsa cruda
2 cloves garlic, crushed
3 medium tomatoes (450g), seeded, chopped finely
1 small brown onion (80g), chopped finely
2 trimmed red radishes (30g), chopped finely
1 lebanese cucumber (130g), chopped finely
2 tablespoons coarsely chopped fresh coriander
1 fresh long red chilli, chopped finely
2 tablespoons lime juice

avocado mash
2 small avocados (400g)
2 tablespoons lime juice

1 Combine oil, juice, oregano, garlic, coriander and cumin in large bowl; add beef, toss to coat in marinade. Cover; refrigerate 3 hours or overnight.

2 Cook beef, capsicums and onion on heated oiled barbecue flat plate until beef is cooked as desired and vegetables are just tender. Cover to keep warm.

3 Meanwhile, make salsa cruda and avocado mash.

4 Make four foil parcels of five tortillas each; heat parcels, both sides, on barbecue flat plate until tortillas are warm and just softened.

5 Cut beef into 1cm slices; combine with cooked vegetables in large bowl. Serve with salsa cruda, avocado mash and tortillas.

salsa cruda Combine ingredients in small bowl.

avocado mash Mash ingredients in small bowl.

preparation time *25 minutes (plus refrigeration time)*
cooking time *15 minutes* serves *4*
nutritional count per serving *46.7g total fat
(9.1g saturated fat); 5321kJ (1273 cal);
134g carbohydrate; 71.6g protein; 13.2g fibre*

tex-mex beef

beef with salsa verde

tex-mex beef

4 x 200g beef scotch fillet steaks
1 medium red capsicum (200g), chopped finely
1 medium yellow capsicum (200g), chopped finely
1 medium green capsicum (200g), chopped finely
1 fresh small red thai chilli, chopped finely
1 tablespoon olive oil
1 tablespoon lime juice

1 Cook beef on heated oiled barbecue until
cooked as desired. Cover beef; stand 5 minutes.

2 Meanwhile, combine capsicums, chilli, oil
and juice in medium bowl. Toss salsa gently;
serve with beef.

preparation time *15 minutes*
cooking time *10 minutes* serves 4
nutritional count per serving *16.7g total fat*
(5.6g saturated fat); 1442kJ (345 cal);
3.8g carbohydrate; 44.2g protein; 1.2g fibre

beef with salsa verde

4 x 200g beef scotch fillet steaks
¼ cup finely chopped fresh flat-leaf parsley
2 tablespoons finely chopped fresh dill
2 tablespoons finely chopped fresh chives
1 tablespoon rinsed, drained baby capers
1 clove garlic, crushed
2 tablespoons olive oil
1 tablespoon lemon juice
2 teaspoons wholegrain mustard

1 Cook beef on heated oiled barbecue until
cooked as desired. Cover beef; stand 5 minutes.

2 Meanwhile, combine remaining ingredients
in small bowl.

3 Serve beef topped with salsa verde.

preparation time *15 minutes*
cooking time *10 minutes* serves 4
nutritional count per serving *21.2g total fat*
(6.3g saturated fat); 1522kJ (364 cal);
0.7g carbohydrate; 42.5g protein; 0.5g fibre

lamb

loin chops rogan josh with pulao salad, page 242

Cook lamb over high heat for medium-rare, or cook for longer over medium heat for well-done. Lamb cutlets are great for the backyard barbie as they are so easy to eat off the bone with no cutlery. Feeding a crowd is easy with large cuts of lamb cooked slowly over indirect heat.

loin chops rogan josh with pulao salad

12 lamb loin chops (1.2kg)
½ cup (150g) rogan josh curry paste
1½ cups (300g) basmati rice
¼ teaspoon ground turmeric
1 cardamom pod, bruised
⅓ cup (45g) roasted slivered almonds
⅓ cup (55g) sultanas
⅓ cup firmly packed fresh coriander leaves
⅓ cup coarsely chopped fresh mint

mustard seed dressing
¼ cup (60ml) olive oil
2 tablespoons yellow mustard seeds
¼ cup (60ml) white wine vinegar
1 tablespoon white sugar

1 Combine lamb and paste in large bowl; turn lamb to coat in paste.

2 Make mustard seed dressing.

3 Cook rice, turmeric and cardamom in large saucepan of boiling water until rice is tender; drain.

4 Meanwhile, cook lamb on heated oiled barbecue until cooked as desired.

5 To make pulao salad, combine rice in large bowl with nuts, sultanas, herbs and dressing. Serve pulao salad with lamb.

mustard seed dressing Heat oil in small saucepan; cook seeds, stirring constantly, over low heat, until aromatic and softened. Place seeds, vinegar and sugar in screw-top jar; shake well.

preparation time *10 minutes*
cooking time *20 minutes* serves *6*
nutritional count per serving *41.6g total fat (11.6g saturated fat); 3072kJ (735 cal); 51.7g carbohydrate; 37.2g protein; 4.2g fibre*

Yellow mustard seeds may also be known as white mustard seeds.

lamb chops with sun-dried tomato pesto

6 lamb chump chops (660g)
½ cup (125ml) lemon juice
½ cup (125ml) dry white wine
2 cloves garlic, crushed

sun-dried tomato pesto
1 cup (150g) drained sun-dried tomatoes in oil
½ cup (125ml) olive oil
½ cup (80g) roasted pine nuts
⅓ cup (25g) grated parmesan cheese
2 tablespoons lemon juice
2 cloves garlic, crushed

1 Trim fat from lamb. Place lamb in shallow dish; pour over combined juice, wine and garlic. Cover; refrigerate 3 hours or overnight.

2 Make sun-dried tomato pesto.

3 Drain lamb; discard marinade. Cook lamb on heated oiled barbecue until cooked as desired.

4 Serve lamb with sun-dried tomato pesto.

sun-dried tomato pesto Blend or process ingredients until combined.

preparation time *15 minutes (plus refrigeration time)*
cooking time *15 minutes* serves *6*
nutritional count per serving *41g total fat (8.7g saturated fat); 2182kJ (522 cal); 10.1g carbohydrate; 23.5g protein; 4.6g fibre*

lamb chops with sun-dried tomato pesto

tandoori lamb with melon and coconut chutney

lamb and chickpea salad

tandoori lamb with melon and coconut chutney

¼ cup (75g) tandoori paste
¼ cup (70g) yogurt
12 french-trimmed lamb cutlets (600g)
1 cup (110g) coarsely grated fresh coconut
½ large firm honeydew melon (850g),
    coarsely grated, drained
2 tablespoons finely chopped fresh mint
1 tablespoon lemon juice

1 Combine paste, yogurt and lamb in large bowl; turn to coat in tandoori mixture. Cook lamb on heated oiled barbecue until cooked as desired.

2 Meanwhile, combine coconut, melon, mint and juice in medium bowl. Serve coconut chutney with lamb and, if desired, pappadums and lemon wedges.

preparation time *15 minutes*
cooking time *10 minutes serves 4*
nutritional count per serving *27.3g total fat*
(13.5g saturated fat); 1601kJ (383 cal);
13.2g carbohydrate; 18.9g protein; 5.7g fibre

To open a fresh coconut, pierce one of the eyes then roast coconut briefly in a very hot oven only until cracks appear in the shell. Cool then break the coconut apart and grate or flake the firm while flesh. If fresh coconut is unavailable, use 1 cup finely shredded dried coconut.

The chutney is best made with a firm (just underripe) honeydew melon.

lamb and chickpea salad

3 cloves garlic, crushed
¼ cup (60ml) lemon juice
1 tablespoon olive oil
2 teaspoons ground cumin
4 x 200g lamb backstraps
2 tablespoons lemon juice, extra
2 tablespoons olive oil, extra
800g can chickpeas, rinsed, drained
3 medium egg tomatoes (225g), cut into wedges
1 lebanese cucumber (130g), halved lengthways,
    sliced thinly
1 medium red onion (170g), sliced thinly
½ cup coarsely chopped fresh mint
½ cup coarsely chopped fresh flat-leaf parsley

1 Combine garlic, juice, oil and cumin in large bowl with lamb. Cover; refrigerate 3 hours or overnight.

2 Drain lamb; reserve marinade. Cook lamb on heated oiled barbecue, brushing occasionally with marinade. Cover lamb; stand 5 minutes then slice thinly.

3 Meanwhile, whisk extra juice and extra oil in large bowl; add remaining ingredients, toss gently. Serve salad topped with lamb.

preparation time *15 minutes (plus refrigeration time)*
cooking time *10 minutes serves 4*
nutritional count per serving *33.2g total fat*
(9.8g saturated fat); 2537kJ (607 cal);
23.3g carbohydrate; 49.5g protein; 9.1g fibre

mongolian lamb cutlets

⅓ cup (80ml) japanese soy sauce
1 tablespoon white sugar
⅓ cup (80ml) dry sherry
1 tablespoon sesame oil
12 french-trimmed lamb cutlets (600g)

1 Combine sauce, sugar, sherry and oil in large bowl; add lamb, turn to coat in marinade. Cover; refrigerate 3 hours or overnight.

2 Drain lamb over medium saucepan; bring marinade to the boil. Reduce heat; simmer, uncovered, until marinade is reduced by half.

3 Meanwhile, cook lamb on heated oiled barbecue until cooked as desired.

4 Serve lamb brushed with marinade.

preparation time *5 minutes (plus refrigeration time)*
cooking time *10 minutes* makes *12*
nutritional count per cutlet 5g *total fat*
(1.8g saturated fat); 318kJ (76 cal);
1.8g carbohydrate; 4.4g protein; 0.1g fibre

lamb chops with capsicum mayonnaise

100g roasted capsicum
½ cup (150g) mayonnaise
8 lamb mid-loin chops (800g)

fetta and olive mash
1kg potatoes, chopped coarsely
⅔ cup (160ml) buttermilk, warmed
200g fetta cheese, crumbled
½ cup thinly sliced black olives
1 tablespoon olive oil

1 Blend or process capsicum and mayonnaise until smooth.

2 Make fetta and olive mash.

3 Meanwhile, cook lamb, on heated oiled barbecue until cooked as desired.

4 Serve lamb with capsicum mayonnaise and fetta and olive mash.

fetta and olive mash Boil, steam or microwave potato until tender; drain. Mash potato in large bowl with buttermilk until smooth. Stir in cheese and olives; drizzle with oil. Cover to keep warm.

preparation time *15 minutes*
cooking time *30 minutes* serves *4*
nutritional count per serving *49.7g total fat*
(19.5g saturated fat); 3420kJ (818 cal);
43.3g carbohydrate; 47.5g protein; 4.2g fibre

If you want to roast your own capsicum, you'll need about 1 medium (200g) red capsicum for the mayonnaise.

mongolian lamb cutlets

lamb chops with capsicum mayonnaise

spanish-style barbecued leg of lamb

moroccan lamb with burghul salad

spanish-style barbecued leg of lamb

2.5kg leg of lamb
2 chorizo sausages (340g), chopped coarsely
10 cloves garlic, halved
1 tablespoon sweet paprika
1 tablespoon olive oil
½ cup (125ml) dry sherry

1 Place lamb in large lightly oiled disposable baking dish. Make deep slits all over lamb with a sharp knife; push sausage and garlic into slits.

2 Combine paprika, oil and sherry in small bowl; rub paprika mixture all over lamb. Cover; refrigerate 3 hours or overnight, turning lamb occasionally.

3 Drain lamb; discard marinade. Cook lamb in covered barbecue, using indirect heat, following manufacturer's instructions about 1 hour 40 minutes or until cooked as desired. Cover lamb; stand 20 minutes before serving.

preparation time *10 minutes*
(plus refrigeration and standing time)
cooking time *1 hour 40 minutes* serves *10*
nutritional count per serving *19.5g total fat*
(8.4g saturated fat); 1547kJ (370 cal);
1g carbohydrate; 45.1g protein; 0.8g fibre

moroccan lamb with burghul salad

¾ cup (120g) burghul
1 tablespoon olive oil
1 tablespoon ras el hanout
4 x 200g lamb backstraps
½ cup (70g) roasted unsalted pistachios, chopped coarsely
1 small red onion (100g), chopped finely
¾ cup loosely packed fresh flat-leaf parsley leaves
¾ cup loosely packed fresh mint leaves
⅓ cup (55g) dried currants
1 tablespoon finely grated lemon rind
1 clove garlic, crushed
¼ cup (60ml) lemon juice
2 tablespoons olive oil, extra

1 Place burghul in medium bowl, cover with water; stand 10 minutes, drain. Squeeze out as much excess water as possible.

2 Combine oil, spice and lamb in medium bowl; turn to coat in mixture. Cook lamb on heated oiled barbecue until cooked as desired. Cover lamb; stand 10 minutes then slice thickly.

3 Combine burghul in medium bowl with remaining ingredients; toss gently.

4 Serve salad topped with sliced lamb. Dollop with yogurt, if desired.

preparation time *20 minutes*
cooking time *20 minutes* serves *4*
nutritional count per serving *30.7g total fat*
(6.3g saturated fat); 2776kJ (664 cal);
38.5g carbohydrate; 53g protein; 10.8g fibre

Ras el hanout is a Moroccan spice blend: allspice, cumin, paprika, fennel, caraway and saffron are all generally part of the mix. It is available from Middle-Eastern food shops and specialty spice stores.

Harissa, a Moroccan sauce or paste made from dried red chillies, garlic, oil and caraway seeds, can be used as a rub for meat, an ingredient in sauces and dressings, or eaten on its own as a condiment. It is available from Middle-Eastern food stores and specialty spice shops.

harissa-scented lamb with vegetables

3 cloves garlic, crushed
1 tablespoon finely grated lemon rind
2 tablespoons harissa
⅓ cup (80ml) lemon juice
1.5kg butterflied leg of lamb, trimmed
2 medium red capsicums (400g), sliced thickly
3 large zucchini (450g), sliced thickly
8 baby eggplants (480g), sliced thickly
1 teaspoon ground cumin
1 tablespoon fresh thyme leaves
½ cup coarsely chopped fresh mint

garlic sauce
1 clove garlic, crushed
1 teaspoon ground cumin
½ cup (125ml) buttermilk
⅓ cup (95g) yogurt

1 Make garlic sauce.

2 Combine garlic, rind, harissa and half the juice in large bowl; add lamb, turn to coat in mixture.

3 Cook lamb in covered barbecue, using indirect heat, following manufacturer's instructions, about 20 minutes or until lamb is cooked as desired. Cover lamb; stand 5 minutes then slice thickly.

4 Combine capsicum, zucchini, eggplant, cumin and remaining juice in large bowl. Cook vegetables on heated oiled barbecue, uncovered, until just tender. Return vegetables to bowl with herbs; toss gently.

5 Serve lamb with char-grilled vegetables; drizzle with garlic sauce.

garlic sauce Combine ingredients in screw-top jar; shake well.

preparation time *20 minutes*
cooking time *30 minutes* serves *6*
nutritional information per serving *7g total fat (3g saturated fat) 1780kJ (354 cal) 9.7g carbohydrate 61.6g protein 4.3g fibre*

lemon garlic lamb with bean, pea and fetta salad

2 tablespoons olive oil
1 tablespoon finely grated lemon rind
2 tablespoons lemon juice
2 cloves garlic, crushed
12 french-trimmed lamb cutlets (600g)
1⅓ cups (225g) frozen broad beans
⅔ cup (80g) frozen baby peas
200g snow peas, trimmed, sliced thinly
1 cup coarsely chopped fresh basil
150g fetta cheese, crumbled
1 cup (150g) seeded kalamata olives

lemon dressing
2 tablespoons lemon juice
¼ cup (60ml) olive oil
1 teaspoon dijon mustard

1 Combine oil, rind, juice and garlic in large bowl; add lamb, turn to coat in mixture.

2 Boil, steam or microwave beans and baby peas, separately, until just tender; drain. Rinse under cold water; drain. Peel away grey-coloured outer shells from broad beans; combine beans and peas in large bowl.

3 Meanwhile, make lemon dressing.

4 Cook lamb on heated oiled barbecue until cooked as desired.

5 Combine snow peas, basil, cheese, olives and half the dressing in bowl with beans and peas; toss gently. Serve salad topped with lamb; drizzle with remaining dressing. Sprinkle with a little finely grated lemon rind, if desired.

lemon dressing Combine ingredients in screw-top jar; shake well.

preparation time 30 minutes
cooking time 15 minutes serves 4
nutritional count per serving 45.2g total fat
(14.9g saturated fat); 2424kJ (580 cal);
17.1g carbohydrate; 27.1g protein; 6.7g fibre

dukkah-crusted cutlets with garlic yogurt

6 cloves garlic, unpeeled
1 teaspoon vegetable oil
1 cup (280g) yogurt
12 french-trimmed lamb cutlets (600g)

dukkah
2 tablespoons roasted hazelnuts
2 tablespoons roasted pistachios
2 tablespoons sesame seeds
2 tablespoons ground coriander
1 tablespoon ground cumin

1 Make dukkah.

2 Place garlic in lightly oiled disposable baking dish; drizzle with oil. Cook garlic in covered barbecue, using indirect heat, following manufacturer's instructions, until soft. Squeeze garlic into small bowl; mash garlic with fork then stir in yogurt. Cover; refrigerate.

3 Press dukkah onto lamb.

4 Cook lamb, on heated oiled barbecue, uncovered, until cooked as desired. Serve lamb with garlic yogurt.

dukkah Blend or process nuts until chopped finely. Dry-fry seeds and spices in small frying pan until fragrant; combine with nuts in medium bowl.

preparation time *10 minutes*
cooking time *20 minutes* serves *4*
nutritional count per serving *27.8g total fat*
(8.7g saturated fat); 1547kJ (370 cal);
5.7g carbohydrate; 22.9g protein; 2.9g fibre

garlic and rosemary smoked lamb

1kg boned rolled lamb loin
4 cloves garlic, halved
8 fresh rosemary sprigs
1 teaspoon dried chilli flakes
1 tablespoon olive oil
handful of smoking chips

1 Place lamb in large shallow dish. Pierce lamb in eight places with sharp knife; push garlic and rosemary into cuts. Sprinkle lamb with chilli; rub with oil. Cover; refrigerate 3 hours or overnight.

2 Place smoking chips in large bowl of water; stand 2 hours.

3 Cook lamb on heated oiled barbecue, uncovered, until browned all over. Place drained chips in smoke box on barbecue next to lamb.

4 Cook lamb in covered barbecue, using indirect heat, following manufacturer's instructions, about 40 minutes or until cooked as desired.

preparation time *10 minutes (plus refrigeration time)*
cooking time *45 minutes* serves *6*
nutritional count per serving *17.8g total fat*
(7.1g saturated fat); 1254kJ (300 cal);
0.2g carbohydrate; 35g; protein; 0.3g fibre

You need smoking chips and a smoke box for this recipe. They are available from specialty barbecue stores.

dukkah-crusted cutlets with garlic yogurt

garlic and rosemary smoked lamb

mediterranean vegetable-filled lamb steaks

teriyaki lamb with carrot salad

mediterranean vegetable-filled lamb steaks

4 butterfly lamb steaks (360g)
8 fresh basil leaves
8 marinated quartered artichoke hearts (100g), drained
⅔ cup (100g) drained semi-dried tomatoes in oil
150g bocconcini cheese, sliced thinly

rocket and red onion salad
2 tablespoons olive oil
1 tablespoon lemon juice
1 teaspoon dijon mustard
100g rocket leaves
½ cup loosely packed fresh basil leaves
1 medium red onion (170g), sliced thinly
1 tablespoon rinsed, drained baby capers

1 Using meat mallet, gently pound lamb between sheets of plastic wrap until 1cm thick. Place two basil leaves on one half of each steak; top each with two artichoke quarters, a quarter of the tomato and a quarter of the cheese. Fold each steak over filling; tie with kitchen string.

2 Cook lamb on heated oiled barbecue until cooked as desired.

3 Meanwhile, make rocket and red onion salad. Serve lamb with salad.

rocket and red onion salad Place oil, juice and mustard in screw-top jar; shake well. Place remaining ingredients in large bowl with dressing; toss gently.

preparation time *25 minutes*
cooking time *15 minutes* serves *4*
nutritional count per serving *25.4g total fat
(9.2g saturated fat); 1672kJ (400 cal);
12g carbohydrate; 30.2g protein; 4.9g fibre*

teriyaki lamb with carrot salad

2 tablespoons japanese soy sauce
2 tablespoons mirin
1 teaspoon caster sugar
600g diced lamb
9 green onions

carrot salad
2 medium carrots (240g), cut into matchsticks
1 cup (80g) bean sprouts
1 small red onion (100g), sliced thinly
1 tablespoon toasted sesame seeds
2 teaspoons japanese soy sauce
1 tablespoon mirin
½ teaspoon white sugar
2 teaspoons peanut oil

1 Combine sauce, mirin and sugar in medium bowl; add lamb, toss to coat in mixture.

2 Cut four 3cm-long pieces from trimmed root end of each onion.

3 Thread lamb and onion pieces, alternately, onto skewers. cook skewers on heated oiled barbecue, brushing with soy mixture occasionally, until lamb is cooked as desired.

4 Meanwhile, make carrot salad. Serve lamb with salad.

carrot salad Combine ingredients in medium bowl.

preparation time *20 minutes*
cooking time *15 minutes* serves *4*
nutritional count per serving *18.4g total fat
(6.8g saturated fat); 1467kJ (351 cal);
7.7g carbohydrate; 35g protein; 3.7g fibre*

You need 12 bamboo skewers for this recipe. Soak them in cold water for about an hour to prevent them from splintering and scorching during cooking.

greek lamb with lemon and potatoes

2kg leg of lamb
3 cloves garlic, quartered
6 sprigs fresh oregano, halved
1 large lemon (180g)
1kg old potatoes, peeled, quartered lengthways
1 teaspoon finely chopped fresh thyme

1 Make 12 small cuts in lamb with a sharp knife. Press garlic and oregano into cuts.

2 Remove rind from lemon; cut rind into long thin strips (or remove rind with a zester). Squeeze juice from lemon (you will need ⅓ cup of juice).

3 Place lamb, upside down, in lightly oiled disposable baking dish; pour juice over lamb. Cover dish lightly with foil; cook in covered barbecue, using indirect heat, following manufacturer's instructions, 2 hours. Turn lamb over; brush all over with pan juices.

4 Add potato to dish; sprinkle with thyme and lemon rind. Cook, covered, further 1¾ hours.

5 Remove foil; cook lamb, uncovered, 15 minutes or until browned. Cover lamb; stand 10 minutes before serving.

preparation time *20 minutes*
cooking time *4 hours* serves *8*
nutritional count per serving *10.1g total fat*
(4.4g saturated fat); 1371kJ (328 cal);
14.2g carbohydrate; 43.6g protein; 2.1g fibre

lamb souvlakia with tomato, mint and almond salad

lamb, capsicum, eggplant and pesto stack

lamb souvlakia with tomato, mint and almond salad

¼ cup (60ml) olive oil
2 teaspoons finely grated lemon rind
¼ cup (60ml) lemon juice
¼ cup finely chopped fresh oregano
800g lamb fillets, cut into 3cm cubes
2 medium yellow capsicums (400g), chopped into cubes
1 medium red onion (150g), chopped coarsely
2 large tomatoes (440g), chopped coarsely
¼ cup (35g) roasted slivered almonds
1 cup firmly packed fresh mint leaves

1   Combine oil, rind, juice and oregano in screw-top jar; shake well.

2   Thread lamb, capsicum and onion, alternately, on skewers. Place on baking tray; drizzle with half the dressing.

3   Cook skewers on heated oiled barbecue until cooked as desired.

4   Meanwhile, combine tomato, nuts and mint with remaining dressing in small bowl.

5   Serve souvlakia with salad, and pitta bread, if desired.

preparation time *20 minutes*
cooking time *15 minutes* serves *4*
nutritional count per serving *26.1g total fat*
(5.5g saturated fat); 1914kJ (458 cal);
7.8g carbohydrate; 46.2g protein; 4.3g fibre

You need 8 bamboo skewers for this recipe. Soak them in water for at least 1 hour before using to prevent them splintering and scorching during cooking.

lamb, capsicum, eggplant and pesto stack

¼ cup (20g) finely grated parmesan cheese
¼ cup (40g) roasted pine nuts
1 clove garlic, quartered
½ cup (125ml) olive oil
1 cup firmly packed fresh basil leaves
1 tablespoon lemon juice
2 medium red capsicums (400g)
1 small eggplant (230g), cut into 8 slices widthways
800g lamb backstraps

1   To make pesto, blend or process cheese, nuts and garlic with half the oil until combined. Add basil and remaining oil; blend until pesto forms a smooth, thick puree. Stir in juice.

2   Quarter capsicums; discard seeds and membranes. Cook capsicum, skin-side down, on heated oiled barbecue until skin blisters and blackens. Cover capsicum pieces with plastic or paper for 5 minutes then peel away skin.

3   Cook eggplant on heated oiled barbecue until tender.

4   Cook lamb on heated oiled barbecue until cooked as desired. Cover lamb; stand 5 minutes then slice thickly.

5   Layer eggplant, lamb and capsicum on plates; spoon pesto over each stack.

preparation time *20 minutes*
cooking time *25 minutes* serves *4*
nutritional count per serving *55.1g total fat*
(13.5g saturated fat); 2959kJ (708 cal);
5.7g carbohydrate; 47.3g protein; 3.5g fibre

lemon grass lamb with vietnamese salad

10cm stick fresh lemon grass (20g), chopped finely
2 tablespoons light soy sauce
1 tablespoon brown sugar
2 tablespoons vegetable oil
600g lamb backstraps
70g rice vermicelli
2 lebanese cucumbers (260g), seeded, sliced thinly
½ small pineapple (450g), chopped coarsely
1 cup (80g) bean sprouts
1 cup loosely packed fresh coriander leaves
1 cup loosely packed fresh mint leaves
1 large carrot (180g), grated coarsely
1 large butter lettuce, trimmed, leaves separated

chilli lime dressing
¼ cup (60ml) hot water
2 tablespoons fish sauce
1 tablespoon brown sugar
2 tablespoons lime juice
2 fresh small red thai chillies, chopped finely
1 clove garlic, crushed

1 Make chilli lime dressing.

2 Combine lemon grass, sauce, sugar and oil in medium bowl; add lamb, turn to coat in mixture.

3 Place vermicelli in medium heatproof bowl, cover with boiling water; stand until just tender, drain. Rinse under cold water; drain.

4 Combine vermicelli in large bowl with cucumber, pineapple, sprouts, herbs, carrot and 2 tablespoons of the dressing; toss gently.

5 Cook lamb on heated oiled barbecue until cooked as desired. Cover lamb; stand 5 minutes then slice thinly.

6 Top lettuce with salad; serve with lamb, drizzle with remaining dressing.

chilli lime dressing Combine ingredients in screw-top jar; shake well.

preparation time 25 minutes
cooking time 20 minutes serves 4
nutritional count per serving 22.9g total fat
(7.2g saturated fat); 1856kJ (444 cal);
20.6g carbohydrate; 35.9g protein; 6g fibre

Sumac is a deep purple-red spice ground from berries that grow on a Mediterranean coastal shrub; it adds a tart, lemony flavour to dips and dressings and goes well with barbecued meat. Sumac can be found in specialty spice stores, Middle-Eastern food stores and major supermarkets.

sumac lamb and vegetable sandwich

1 tablespoon lemon juice
1 tablespoon sumac
1 clove garlic, crushed
¼ cup (60ml) olive oil
400g lamb backstraps
1 small eggplant (230g), sliced thinly lengthways
1 small yellow capsicum (150g), sliced thickly
1 small red onion (100g), sliced thickly
2 small tomatoes (180g), sliced thickly
1 tablespoon balsamic vinegar
40g baby spinach leaves
⅓ cup loosely packed fresh flat-leaf parsley leaves
100g haloumi cheese, cut into four slices
4 ciabatta bread rolls (400g), halved
⅓ cup (80g) hummus

1 Combine juice, sumac, garlic and 1 tablespoon of the oil in medium bowl; add lamb, turn to coat in marinade.

2 Combine eggplant, capsicum, onion, tomato and vinegar with remaining oil in large shallow lightly oiled disposable baking dish. Cook vegetables in covered barbecue, using indirect heat, following manufacturer's instructions, about 25 minutes or until tender. Place vegetables in medium bowl with spinach and parsley; toss gently, cover to keep warm.

3 Cook lamb on heated oiled barbecue, uncovered, until cooked as desired. Cover lamb; stand 5 minutes then slice thinly.

4 Cook cheese on heated oiled barbecue, uncovered, until browned both sides. Drain on absorbent paper.

5 Toast rolls on heated oiled barbecue.

6 Spread hummus on each roll half; top with lamb, vegetable mixture, cheese then other roll half.

preparation time *20 minutes*
cooking time *25 minutes* serves *4*
nutritional count per serving *14.7g total fat (5.5g saturated fat); 2516kJ (605 cal); 82.8g carbohydrate; 26.3g protein; 2.6g fibre*

lamb burgers with beetroot relish and yogurt

500g lamb mince
1 small brown onion (80g), chopped finely
2 cloves garlic, crushed
1 teaspoon ground cumin
1 egg, beaten lightly
¾ cup (210g) yogurt
½ teaspoon ground cumin, extra
1 tablespoon finely chopped fresh mint
1 long loaf turkish bread (430g)
50g baby rocket leaves

beetroot relish
⅓ cup (80ml) water
4 medium beetroot (700g), trimmed, grated coarsely
1 small brown onion (80g), chopped finely
½ cup (110g) white sugar
⅔ cup (160ml) cider vinegar

1 Make beetroot relish.

2 Meanwhile, combine lamb, onion, garlic, cumin and egg in medium bowl; shape mixture into four patties.

3 Cook patties on heated oiled barbecue until cooked through. Cover to keep warm.

4 Combine yogurt, extra cumin and mint in small bowl.

5 Cut bread into quarters; halve quarters horizontally. Toast bread on heated oiled barbecue.

6 Sandwich rocket, patties, yogurt mixture and relish between toast pieces.

beetroot relish Combine the water, beetroot and onion in large frying pan; cook, covered, about 15 minutes or until beetroot is tender. Stir in sugar and vinegar; cook, covered, stirring occasionally, 20 minutes. Uncover; cook, stirring occasionally, about 10 minutes or until liquid evaporates.

preparation time *30 minutes*
cooking time *45 minutes* serves *4*
nutritional count per serving *22g total fat
(7.9g saturated fat); 3173kJ (759 cal);
95.9g carbohydrate; 43.6g protein; 8.6g fibre*

Beetroot relish will keep, covered and refrigerated, for up to three days.

greek lamb cutlets with skordalia

lamb with mint pesto

greek lamb cutlets with skordalia

1 tablespoon finely chopped fresh thyme
1 tablespoon finely grated lemon rind
2 teaspoons ground black pepper
2 tablespoons olive oil
2 tablespoons lemon juice
4 cloves garlic, crushed
12 french-trimmed lamb cutlets (600g)
1 slice day-old white bread, crust removed
⅓ cup (80g) mashed potato
12 sprigs fresh thyme

1 Combine chopped thyme, rind, pepper, half the oil, half the juice and half the garlic in large bowl; add lamb, turn to coat in marinade. Cover; refrigerate 3 hours or overnight.

2 Make skordalia by cutting bread into quarters; soak in small bowl of cold water 2 minutes. Squeeze as much water from bread as possible. Blend or process bread, potato, and remaining juice and garlic until smooth. With motor operating, add remaining oil in a thin steady stream; process until skordalia thickens.

3 Cook lamb, on heated oiled barbecue until cooked as desired.

4 Serve lamb topped with skordalia and thyme sprigs.

preparation time *20 minutes (plus refrigeration time)*
cooking time *10 minutes* serves *4*
nutritional count per serving *20.2g total fat
(6.2g saturated fat); 1087kJ (260 cal);
6.1g carbohydrate; 13.5g protein; 1.3g fibre*

Skordalia, the classic Greek accompaniment for grilled meats or seafood, is made from mashed potato and/or white bread pureed with garlic, olive oil and lemon juice or vinegar.

lamb with mint pesto

2 cups firmly packed fresh mint leaves
2 cloves garlic, quartered
⅓ cup (45g) roasted unsalted pistachios
⅓ cup (80ml) olive oil
2 tablespoons coarsely grated parmesan cheese
4 x 200g lamb backstraps

1 To make pesto, blend or process mint, garlic, nuts, oil and cheese until mixture forms a paste.

2 Cook lamb on heated oiled barbecue until cooked as desired. Cover lamb; stand 5 minutes.

3 Serve lamb with mint pesto, and sliced boiled baby new potatoes, if desired.

preparation time *15 minutes*
cooking time *10 minutes* serves *4*
nutritional count per serving *32g total fat
(7.1g saturated fat); 2019kJ (483 cal);
2.8g carbohydrate; 45.2g protein; 3.6g fibre*

gözleme

4 cups (600g) plain flour
1 teaspoon coarse cooking salt
1⅔ cups (410ml) warm water
2 tablespoons vegetable oil

spinach and cheese filling
300g spinach, trimmed, shredded finely
½ cup coarsely chopped fresh mint
1 small brown onion (80g), chopped finely
½ teaspoon ground allspice
250g fetta cheese, crumbled
1 cup (100g) coarsely grated mozzarella cheese

lamb filling
1 tablespoon vegetable oil
2 teaspoons ground cumin
½ teaspoon hot paprika
3 cloves garlic, crushed
500g lamb mince
410g can chopped tomatoes
½ cup coarsely chopped fresh flat-leaf parsley

1   Combine flour and salt in large bowl. Gradually stir in the water; mix to a soft dough. Knead dough on floured surface about 5 minutes or until smooth and elastic. Return to bowl; cover.

2   Make spinach and cheese filling. Make lamb filling.

3   Divide dough into six pieces; roll each piece into 30cm square. Divide spinach and cheese filling equally among dough squares, spreading filling across centre of squares; top each with equal amounts of lamb filling. Fold top and bottom edges of dough over filling; tuck in ends to enclose.

4   Cook gözleme on heated oiled barbecue, over low heat, brushing with oil, until browned lightly both sides and heated through.

spinach and cheese filling   Combine ingredients in medium bowl.

lamb filling   Heat oil in large frying pan; cook spices and garlic until fragrant. Add lamb; cook, stirring, until browned. Add undrained tomatoes; simmer about 15 minutes or until liquid is almost evaporated. Stir in parsley.

preparation time *50 minutes*
cooking time *40 minutes* serves *6*
nutritional count per serving *29.9g total fat (12.7g saturated fat); 3168kJ (758 cal); 75.8g carbohydrate; 41.8g protein; 7.1g fibre*

Gözleme (pronounced goz-LEH-meh), from Anatolia in Turkey, is a centuries-old village dish made of flat bread folded around various ingredients then cooked on a grill or griddle. Traditionally, gözleme, being an economical peasant dish, contains less meat filling than ours.

lamb yakitori

½ cup (125ml) japanese soy sauce
½ cup (125ml) sake
¼ cup (60ml) mirin
2 tablespoons white sugar
500g diced lamb
1 medium carrot (120g), sliced thinly
6 green onions, cut into 3cm lengths

1 Bring sauce, sake, mirin and sugar to the boil in small saucepan. Reduce heat; simmer, uncovered, until sauce reduces by a third. Cool 10 minutes.

2 Meanwhile, thread lamb, carrot and onion, alternately, onto skewers.

3 Cook skewers on heated oiled barbecue brushing with half the sauce occasionally, until browned all over and cooked as desired. Serve yakitori with remaining sauce.

preparation time *20 minutes*
cooking time *20 minutes* serves *4*
nutritional count per serving *11.1g total fat (5g saturated fat); 1229kJ (294 cal); 12.1g carbohydrate; 28.4g protein; 1.1g fibre*

You need 8 bamboo skewers for this recipe. Soak them in cold water for at least 1 hour before using to prevent them splintering and scorching during cooking.

lamb wrapped in prosciutto with herb risotto

4 x 200g lamb backstraps
1 tablespoon sun-dried tomato pesto
8 slices prosciutto (120g)
1 litre (4 cups) chicken stock
½ cup (125ml) dry white wine
1 tablespoon olive oil
1 medium brown onion (150g), chopped finely
1 clove garlic, crushed
1½ cups (300g) arborio rice
⅓ cup (25g) finely grated parmesan cheese
⅓ cup loosely packed fresh chervil leaves
2 tablespoons fresh tarragon leaves
2 tablespoons finely chopped fresh chives
300g mushrooms, sliced thickly

1 Rub one side of each backstrap with one teaspoon of the pesto. Wrap each backstrap with two slices of prosciutto.

2 Combine stock and wine in medium saucepan; bring to the boil. Reduce heat; simmer, covered.

3 Heat oil in large saucepan; cook onion and garlic, stirring, until onion softens. Add rice; stir rice to coat in oil mixture. Stir in 1 cup simmering stock mixture; cook, stirring, over low heat, until liquid is absorbed. Continue adding stock mixture, in 1 cup batches, stirring, until liquid is absorbed after each addition. Total cooking time should be about 35 minutes or until rice is just tender. Stir in cheese and herbs.

4 Meanwhile, cook lamb on heated oiled barbecue until cooked as desired. Cover lamb; stand 5 minutes then slice thickly.

5 Cook mushrooms on heated oiled barbecue until tender.

6 Serve lamb with risotto and mushrooms.

preparation time *10 minutes*
cooking time *35 minutes* serves *4*
nutritional count per serving *19.2g total fat (6.8g saturated fat); 2918kJ (698 cal); 63.7g carbohydrate; 60.4g protein; 3.3g fibre*

lamb yakitori

lamb wrapped in prosciutto with herb risotto

kofta with tunisian carrot salad

rosemary and garlic kebabs

kofta with tunisian carrot salad

500g lamb mince
1 cup (70g) fresh breadcrumbs
¼ cup finely chopped fresh mint
1 teaspoon ground allspice
1 teaspoon ground coriander
1 teaspoon cracked black pepper
1 tablespoon lemon juice
¾ cup (200g) yogurt

tunisian carrot salad
3 large carrots (540g)
¼ cup (60ml) lemon juice
1 tablespoon olive oil
½ teaspoon ground cinnamon
½ teaspoon ground coriander
¼ cup firmly packed fresh mint leaves
¼ cup (35g) roasted pistachios
¼ cup (40g) sultanas

1 Combine lamb, breadcrumbs, mint, spices and juice in medium bowl; roll mixture into 12 balls, roll balls into sausage-shaped kofta.

2 Cook kofta on heated oiled barbecue until cooked through.

3 Meanwhile, make tunisian carrot salad. Serve kofta with salad and yogurt.

tunisian carrot salad Cut carrot into 5cm pieces; slice pieces thinly lengthways. Cook carrot on heated oiled barbecue until just tender. Place carrot in large bowl with remaining ingredients; toss gently.

preparation time *15 minutes*
cooking time *15 minutes* serves *4*
nutritional count per serving *20g total fat (6.2g saturated fat); 1873kJ (448 cal); 30g carbohydrate; 33.8g protein; 6.5g fibre*

rosemary and garlic kebabs

8 x 15cm stalks fresh rosemary
1 clove garlic, crushed
1 tablespoon lemon juice
1 tablespoon olive oil
500g diced lamb

1 Pull enough leaves from bottom of rosemary stalks to make 2 tablespoons of finely chopped leaves; toss in small bowl with garlic, juice and oil.

2 Thread lamb onto rosemary stalk skewers; brush with rosemary oil mixture.

3 Cook kebabs on heated oiled barbecue until cooked as desired.

preparation time *20 minutes*
cooking time *20 minutes* serves *4*
nutritional count per serving *15.6g total fat (5.7g saturated fat); 1024kJ (245 cal); 0.3g carbohydrate; 26.2g protein; 0.1g fibre*

You can pierce with lamb with metal or bamboo skewers first to make threading the rosemary stalks easier.

moroccan lamb leg with fruity couscous

2 tablespoons ras el hanout
2 tablespoons olive oil
1.5kg butterflied lamb leg

fruity couscous
1½ cups (375ml) water
1½ cups (300g) couscous
2 medium oranges (480g)
1 cup (230g) fresh dates, seeded, quartered
1 cup (100g) roasted walnuts, chopped coarsely
⅓ cup coarsely chopped fresh flat-leaf parsley
½ cup (125ml) orange juice
2 tablespoons walnut oil
½ teaspoon ground cinnamon

1 Combine ras el hanout and oil in large bowl; add lamb, turn to coat in marinade. Cover; refrigerate 3 hours or overnight.

2 Cook lamb in covered barbecue, using indirect heat, following manufacturer's instructions, about 35 minutes or until cooked through, turning midway through cooking time. Cover lamb; stand 10 minutes then slice thickly.

3 Meanwhile, make fruity couscous.

4 Serve lamb with couscous.

fruity couscous Place the water in medium saucepan; bring to the boil, remove from heat. Stir in couscous. Cover; stand about 5 minutes or until liquid is absorbed, fluffing occasionally with fork. Segment oranges over pan. Add orange and remaining ingredients; mix gently.

preparation time *25 minutes (plus refrigeration time)* cooking time *35 minutes* serves *6*
nutritional count per serving *37.6g total fat (8.1g saturated fat); 3490kJ (835 cal); 57.4g carbohydrate; 65.2g protein; 4.6g fibre*

With a name that loosely translates as "top of the shop", ras el hanout is a Moroccan blend of the best a spice merchant has to offer: allspice, cumin, paprika, fennel, caraway and saffron are all generally part of the mix. It is available from Middle-Eastern food shops and specialty spice stores.

sesame, chilli and parsley lamb

lamb with pecan tomato salsa

sesame, chilli and parsley lamb

½ cup (75g) toasted sesame seeds
½ teaspoon dried chilli flakes
2 tablespoons finely chopped fresh flat-leaf parsley
4 x 200g lamb backstraps
2 tablespoons olive oil

1 Combine seeds, chilli and parsley in small bowl.

2 Combine lamb with oil in large bowl; add sesame mixture, turn lamb to coat all over.

3 Cook lamb on heated oiled barbecue until cooked as desired. Cover lamb; stand 5 minutes then slice thickly.

preparation time 15 minutes
cooking time 10 minutes serves 4
nutritional count per serving 26.7g total fat
(5.8g saturated fat); 1772kJ (424 cal);
0.2g carbohydrate; 45.2g protein; 2g fibre

lamb with pecan tomato salsa

4 x 200g lamb backstraps
2 tablespoons olive oil
2 tablespoons balsamic vinegar
1 clove garlic, crushed
2 teaspoons grated lemon rind
1 cup (125g) coarsely chopped roasted pecans
2 small tomatoes (180g), seeded, chopped coarsely
1 medium red onion (170g), chopped coarsely
½ cup coarsely chopped fresh flat-leaf parsley

1 Cook lamb on heated oiled barbecue until browned all over and cooked as desired. Cover; stand 5 minutes then slice thickly.

2 Meanwhile, combine remaining ingredients in medium bowl. Serve lamb with salsa.

preparation time 20 minutes
cooking time 10 minutes serves 4
nutritional count per serving 38.9g total fat
(5.9g saturated fat); 2320kJ (555 cal);
4.8g carbohydrate; 45.3g protein; 4.3g fibre

pork

281

pork chops with kumara and cranberry salad, page 284

Like chicken, pork should be cooked over moderately-low heat around the edge of the barbecue. Cuts with bones, like that perennial favourite, marinated pork spareribs, are especially tasty and moist.

pork chops with kumara and cranberry salad

1 tablespoon ground ginger
1 tablespoon ground coriander
1 teaspoon sweet paprika
½ cup (160g) cranberry sauce
2 tablespoons orange juice
2 tablespoons lemon juice
1 tablespoon dijon mustard
4 x 280g pork loin chops

kumara and cranberry salad
3 large kumara (1.5kg), cut into 2cm pieces
2 tablespoons olive oil
½ cup (80g) roasted pine nuts
⅓ cup (50g) dried cranberries
1 cup coarsely chopped fresh coriander
¼ cup (60ml) white wine vinegar
2 teaspoons olive oil, extra

1 Combine ginger, coriander, paprika, sauce, juices and mustard in large bowl; add pork, toss to coat in mixture.

2 Make kumara and cranberry salad.

3 Cook pork on heated oiled barbecue until browned and cooked through. Serve pork with salad.

kumara cranberry salad Boil, steam or microwave kumara until just tender; drain. Combine kumara with oil in large bowl; cook kumara on heated oiled barbecue until browned lightly. Return kumara to same bowl with remaining ingredients; toss gently.

preparation time *15 minutes*
cooking time *30 minutes* serves *4*
nutritional count per serving *48.1g total fat (10g saturated fat); 3921kJ (938 cal); 73.3g carbohydrate; 49.3g protein; 8g fibre*

spiced pork cutlets with carrot and olive salad

2 tablespoons olive oil
¼ cup (60ml) lemon juice
2 teaspoons ground cumin
1 tablespoon sweet paprika
4 x 250g pork cutlets

carrot and olive salad
4 medium carrots (480g), halved lengthways, sliced thinly
1 cup (120g) seeded black olives, chopped coarsely
½ cup loosely packed fresh flat-leaf parsley leaves
½ cup loosely packed fresh coriander leaves
2 tablespoons olive oil
2 teaspoons ground cumin
1 tablespoon red wine vinegar
2 teaspoons harissa

1 Combine oil, juice, cumin and paprika in large bowl; add pork, toss to coat in mixture.

2 Meanwhile, make carrot and olive salad.

3 Cook pork on heated oiled barbecue until cooked through.

4 Serve pork with salad.

carrot and olive salad Boil, steam or microwave carrot until just tender; drain. Cool 10 minutes. Place carrot in medium bowl with olives, herbs and combined remaining ingredients; toss gently.

preparation time *20 minutes*
cooking time *20 minutes* serves *4*
nutritional count per serving *36.2g total fat (8.6g saturated fat); 2123kJ (508 cal); 13g carbohydrate; 31.3g protein; 4.4g fibre*

spiced pork cutlets with carrot and olive salad

pork cutlets with fennel apple relish

glazed pork cutlets with celeriac salad

pork cutlets with fennel apple relish

2 tablespoons cider vinegar
¼ cup (60ml) olive oil
1 tablespoon dijon mustard
2 teaspoons caster sugar
4 x 250g pork cutlets
1 large unpeeled green apple (200g), chopped finely
1 small red onion (100g), chopped finely
1 medium fennel bulb (300g), trimmed, chopped finely

crushed potato
1kg baby new potatoes, unpeeled
½ cup (120g) sour cream
40g butter, softened
2 tablespoons coarsely chopped fresh dill
¼ cup coarsely chopped fresh flat-leaf parsley

1 Whisk vinegar, oil, mustard and sugar in medium bowl. Transfer 2 tablespoons of the dressing to large bowl; add pork, turn to coat in dressing.

2 To make relish, combine apple, onion and fennel in medium bowl with remaining dressing.

3 Make crushed potato.

4 Drain pork; reserve dressing. Cook pork on heated oiled barbecue until cooked through, brushing occasionally with reserved dressing.

5 Serve pork with relish and crushed potato.

crushed potato Boil, steam or microwave potatoes until tender; drain. Mash half the potatoes with sour cream and butter in large bowl until smooth; stir in dill and parsley. Roughly crush remaining potatoes with back of fork until skins burst and flesh is just crushed; stir into herbed mash.

preparation time 15 minutes
cooking time 20 minutes serves 4
nutritional count per serving 52.2g total fat
(21.5g saturated fat); 3394kJ (811 cal);
43.6g carbohydrate; 38.8g protein; 7.3g fibre

glazed pork cutlets with celeriac salad

2 teaspoons honey
1 teaspoon dijon mustard
1 tablespoon olive oil
4 x 250g pork cutlets
400g baby carrots, trimmed
650g celeriac, grated coarsely
⅓ cup (100g) mayonnaise
1 clove garlic, crushed
⅓ cup (80g) light sour cream
2 tablespoons lemon juice
½ cup coarsely chopped fresh flat-leaf parsley
2 teaspoons dijon mustard, extra

1 Whisk honey, mustard and oil in large bowl; add pork, toss to coat in mixture. Cook pork on heated oiled barbecue until cooked through. Cover pork; stand 5 minutes.

2 Meanwhile, boil, steam or microwave carrots until just tender; drain. Cover to keep warm.

3 Combine celeriac, mayonnaise, garlic, sour cream, juice, parsley and extra mustard in medium bowl.

4 Serve cutlets with carrots and celeriac salad.

preparation time 5 minutes
cooking time 15 minutes serves 4
nutritional count per serving 37.8g total fat
(9.6g saturated fat); 2441kJ (584 cal);
15.5g carbohydrate; 45.6g protein; 9g fibre

asian pork and apple salad

⅓ cup (80ml) hoisin sauce
1 tablespoon fish sauce
1 tablespoon light soy sauce
2 tablespoons rice vinegar
¼ cup (90g) honey
½ teaspoon five-spice powder
2 cloves garlic, crushed
2cm piece fresh ginger (10g), grated
800g pork fillets, halved
1 tablespoon water
½ medium iceberg lettuce, chopped coarsely
50g bean sprouts
1 small red onion (100g), sliced thinly
1 medium green apple (150g), unpeeled, sliced thinly
⅓ cup firmly packed fresh mint leaves

1 Combine sauces, vinegar, honey, five-spice, garlic and ginger in medium jug. Combine ½ cup of the sauce mixture in medium bowl with pork. Cover; refrigerate 3 hours or overnight. Stir the water into remaining sauce mixture; refrigerate.

2 Drain pork; reserve marinade. Cook pork on heated oiled barbecue, brushing occasionally with marinade until cooked through. Cover pork; stand 10 minutes then slice thickly.

3 Combine remaining ingredients in medium bowl. Top salad with pork; serve with reserved sauce.

preparation time *20 minutes (plus refrigeration time)*
cooking time *20 minutes* serves 4
nutritional count per serving *16.4g total fat (5.3g saturated fat); 1923kJ (460 cal); 32.4g carbohydrate; 42.6g protein; 5.4g fibre*

jerk pork cutlets with pumpkin chips

mexican pork cutlets with avocado salsa

jerk pork cutlets with pumpkin chips

3 long green chillies, chopped coarsely
3 green onions, chopped coarsely
2 cloves garlic, crushed
1 teaspoon ground allspice
1 teaspoon dried thyme
1 teaspoon white sugar
1 tablespoon light soy sauce
1 tablespoon lime juice
4 x 280g pork loin chops
1kg piece pumpkin, trimmed
2 tablespoons vegetable oil

piri piri dipping sauce
⅓ cup (100g) mayonnaise
2 tablespoons piri piri sauce

1 Combine chilli, onion, garlic, allspice, thyme, sugar, sauce, juice and pork in medium bowl.

2 Make piri piri dipping sauce.

3 Cut pumpkin into 7cm chips; boil, steam or microwave until tender; drain. Combine pumpkin with the oil in medium bowl; cook on heated oiled barbecue until browned.

4 Cook pork on heated oiled barbecue until cooked through. Serve pork with pumpkin chips and dipping sauce.

piri piri dipping sauce Combine ingredients in small bowl.

preparation time *15 minutes*
cooking time *25 minutes* serves *4*
nutritional count per serving *39g total fat (9.8g saturated fat); 2554kJ (611 cal); 21.6g carbohydrate; 42.1g protein; 3.6g fibre*

mexican pork cutlets with avocado salsa

2 tablespoons taco seasoning mix
¼ cup (60ml) olive oil
4 x 250g pork cutlets
3 small tomatoes (270g), seeded, chopped finely
1 small avocado (200g), chopped finely
1 lebanese cucumber (130g), seeded, chopped finely
1 tablespoon lime juice

1 Combine seasoning, 2 tablespoons of the oil and pork in large bowl.

2 Cook pork on heated oiled barbecue until cooked through.

3 Meanwhile, combine remaining oil in medium bowl with tomato, avocado, cucumber and juice. Serve pork with salsa.

preparation time *10 minutes*
cooking time *10 minutes* serves *4*
nutritional count per serving *42.2g total fat (10.7g saturated fat); 2241kJ (536 cal); 1.2g carbohydrate; 38g protein; 1.2g fibre*

Found in most supermarkets, sachets of taco seasoning mix are meant to duplicate the taste of a Mexican sauce made from cumin, oregano, chillies and other spices.

five-spice pork ribs with crunchy noodle salad

3 cloves garlic, crushed
3cm piece fresh ginger (15g), grated
1½ teaspoons five-spice powder
¼ cup (85g) orange marmalade
¼ cup (90g) honey
2 tablespoons kecap manis
1.5kg pork belly ribs

crunchy noodle salad
10 trimmed red radishes (150g), sliced thinly
1 large red capsicum (350g), sliced thinly
½ small wombok (350g), shredded finely
6 green onions, chopped finely
100g packet fried noodles
¼ cup (60ml) white vinegar
¼ cup (55g) brown sugar
¼ cup (60ml) soy sauce
2 teaspoons sesame oil
1 clove garlic, crushed

1 Combine garlic, ginger, five-spice, marmalade, honey and kecap manis in large bowl; add pork, toss pork to coat in marinade. Cover; refrigerate 3 hours or overnight.

2 Drain pork; reserve marinade. Cook pork on heated oiled barbecue, brushing occasionally with reserved marinade, until cooked through.

3 Meanwhile, make crunchy noodle salad. Serve pork with salad.

crunchy noodle salad Combine radish, capsicum, wombok, onion and noodles in large bowl. Combine remaining ingredients in screw-top jar; shake well. Pour dressing over salad; toss gently.

preparation time *20 minutes (plus refrigeration time)*
cooking time *20 minutes* serves *4*
nutritional count per serving *43.4g total fat
(14.6g saturated fat); 3227kJ (772 cal);
57.7g carbohydrate; 36.2g protein; 3.9g fibre*

teriyaki pork with pineapple

loin chops with apple and onion plum sauce

teriyaki pork with pineapple

⅓ cup (80ml) mirin
¼ cup (60ml) japanese soy sauce
2 tablespoons cooking sake
2 teaspoons white sugar
5cm piece fresh ginger (25g), grated
2 cloves garlic, crushed
800g pork fillets
1 small pineapple (900g), sliced thinly
2 green onions, sliced thinly

1 Combine mirin, sauce, sake, sugar, ginger and garlic in large bowl; add pork, turn to coat in marinade. Cover; refrigerate 3 hours or overnight.

2 Drain pork; reserve marinade. Cook pork on heated oiled barbecue until browned and cooked through. Cover pork; stand 10 minutes then slice thickly.

3 Cook pineapple on heated oiled barbecue about 2 minutes or until soft.

4 Bring reserved marinade to the boil in small saucepan; cook about 5 minutes or until sauce reduces by half.

5 Serve sliced pork with pineapple and onion; drizzle with sauce.

preparation time *20 minutes (plus refrigeration time)*
cooking time *20 minutes* serves *4*
nutritional count per serving *12.2g total fat
(4.1g saturated fat); 1371kJ (328 cal);
13.3g carbohydrate; 34.1g protein; 3g fibre*

loin chops with apple and onion plum sauce

2 medium apples (300g)
1 medium red onion (170g),
    cut into thin wedges
4 x 280g pork loin chops
½ cup (125ml) plum sauce
¼ cup (60ml) lemon juice
⅓ cup (80ml) chicken stock

1 Cut each unpeeled, uncored apple horizontally into four slices. Cook apple and onion on heated oiled barbecue grill plate, turning, until softened.

2 Meanwhile, cook pork on heated oiled barbecue until cooked through.

3 Stir sauce, juice and stock into apple mixture; simmer, uncovered, 1 minute. Serve pork with sauce.

preparation time *10 minutes*
cooking time *20 minutes* serves *4*
nutritional count per serving *29.7g total fat
(9.1g saturated fat); 2404kJ (575 cal);
32g carbohydrate; 45g protein; 1.8g fibre*

sticky pork spareribs

1 teaspoon sesame oil
3 cloves garlic, crushed
4cm piece fresh ginger (20g), grated
2 teaspoons five-spice powder
⅓ cup (115g) marmalade
⅓ cup (120g) honey
¼ cup (60ml) kecap manis
3kg american-style pork spareribs

1 Combine oil, garlic, ginger, five-spice, marmalade, honey and kecap manis in large bowl; add ribs, turn to coat in marinade. Cover; refrigerate 3 hours or overnight.

2 Drain ribs over medium bowl; reserve marinade. Cook ribs on heated oiled barbecue, turning and brushing with marinade occasionally, until cooked through.

preparation time *10 minutes (plus refrigeration time)*
cooking time *30 minutes* serves *8*
nutritional count per serving *29.3g total fat (11.4g saturated fat); 2224kJ (532 cal); 22.2g carbohydrate; 46.1g protein; 0.4g fibre*

texan-style spareribs

3kg american-style pork spareribs
2 tablespoons sweet paprika
1 tablespoon ground cumin
1 teaspoon cayenne pepper
2 x 800ml bottles beer
1 cup (250ml) barbecue sauce
¼ cup (60ml) water
¼ cup (60ml) maple syrup
¼ cup (60ml) cider vinegar

1 Place ribs on large tray. Combine spices in small bowl; rub spice mixture all over ribs. Cover; refrigerate 3 hours or overnight.

2 Bring beer to the boil in medium saucepan. Reduce heat; simmer, uncovered, 20 minutes. Divide beer and ribs between two large shallow disposable baking dishes; cook in covered barbecue, using indirect heat, following manufacturer's instructions, for 1½ hours. Remove from oven; discard beer.

3 Meanwhile, combine sauce, the water, syrup and vinegar in small saucepan; bring to the boil. Reduce heat; simmer, uncovered, 5 minutes.

4 Cook ribs, in batches, on heated oiled barbecue, uncovered, turning and brushing with sauce occasionally, until browned all over.

preparation time *20 minutes (plus refrigeration time)*
cooking time *2 hours 5 minutes* serves *8*
nutritional count per serving *17.5g total fat (6.1g saturated fat); 2123kJ (508 cal); 25.4g carbohydrate; 49.8g protein; 0.4g fibre*

sticky pork spareribs

texan-style spareribs

pork fillets with gnocchi salad

pork medallions with capsicum cream sauce

pork fillets with gnocchi salad

1 tablespoon olive oil
1 tablespoon balsamic vinegar
1 clove garlic, crushed
800g pork fillets
1 medium red onion (170g), cut into wedges
1 medium red capsicum (200g), quartered
1 medium yellow capsicum (200g), quartered
500g packet potato gnocchi
250g grape tomatoes, halved
1 cup loosely packed fresh basil leaves, torn
1 cup (150g) seeded kalamata olives

balsamic dressing
2 tablespoons olive oil
2 tablespoons balsamic vinegar
1 clove garlic, crushed
1 teaspoon dijon mustard

1   Combine oil, vinegar and garlic in large bowl; add pork, toss to coat in mixture.

2   Meanwhile, make balsamic dressing.

3   Cook onion and capsicums on heated oiled barbecue until tender; slice capsicums thickly. Place onion and capsicums in large bowl; cover to keep warm.

4   Meanwhile, cook gnocchi in large saucepan of boiling water, uncovered, until gnocchi float to the surface. Remove from pan with slotted spoon; place in bowl with grilled vegetables.

5   Cook pork on heated oiled barbecue until cooked as desired. Cover pork; stand 5 minutes then slice thickly.

6   Add dressing, tomato, basil and olives to bowl with grilled vegetables and gnocchi; toss gently. Serve pork with salad.

balsamic dressing Combine ingredients in screw-top jar; shake well.

preparation time *15 minutes*
cooking time *25 minutes* serves *4*
nutritional count per serving *20.1g total fat (4.1g saturated fat); 2546kJ (609 cal); 51.4g carbohydrate; 51.9g protein; 6.4g fibre*

pork medallions with capsicum cream sauce

1 medium red capsicum (200g)
1 medium tomato (150g), halved, seeded
2 teaspoons olive oil
1 clove garlic, crushed
1 small brown onion (80g), chopped finely
½ trimmed celery stalk (50g), chopped finely
2 tablespoons water
1 teaspoon finely chopped fresh rosemary
4 x 150g pork medallions
½ cup (125ml) cream

1   Quarter capsicum; discard seeds and membranes. Cook capsicum, skin-side down, and tomato on heated oiled barbecue, uncovered, until capsicum skin blisters and blackens. Cover capsicum and tomato pieces with plastic or paper for 5 minutes then peel away skins. Slice capsicum thickly.

2   Heat oil in large frying pan; cook garlic, onion and celery, uncovered, until softened. Add capsicum, tomato and the water; cook, 5 minutes. Remove from heat; stir in rosemary.

3   Meanwhile, cook pork on heated oiled barbecue until cooked through. Cover to keep warm.

4   Blend or process capsicum mixture until smooth. Return to pan, add cream; bring to the boil. Reduce heat; simmer, uncovered, 5 minutes. Serve pork with sauce.

preparation time *15 minutes*
cooking time *15 minutes* serves *4*
nutritional count per serving *19.4g total fat (10.5g saturated fat); 1404kJ (336 cal); 4.7g carbohydrate; 35g protein; 1.8g fibre*

pork spareribs with red cabbage coleslaw

2kg american-style pork spareribs

barbecue sauce
1 cup (250ml) tomato sauce
¾ cup (180ml) cider vinegar
2 tablespoons olive oil
¼ cup (60ml) worcestershire sauce
⅓ cup (75g) firmly packed brown sugar
2 tablespoons american mustard
1 teaspoon cracked black pepper
2 fresh small red thai chillies, chopped finely
2 cloves garlic, crushed
2 tablespoons lemon juice

red cabbage coleslaw
½ cup (120g) sour cream
¼ cup (60ml) lemon juice
2 tablespoons water
½ small red cabbage (600g), shredded finely
3 green onions, sliced thinly

1 Make barbecue sauce.

2 Place ribs in large shallow disposable baking dish. Pour sauce over ribs, cover; refrigerate 3 hours or overnight, turning ribs occasionally.

3 Make red cabbage coleslaw.

4 Drain ribs; reserve sauce. Cook ribs on heated oiled barbecue, brushing occasionally with reserved sauce, about 15 minutes or until cooked. Turn ribs midway through cooking time.

5 Bring reserved sauce to the boil in small saucepan; cook about 4 minutes or until sauce thickens slightly.

6 Cut ribs into serving-sized pieces; serve with hot barbecue sauce and red cabbage coleslaw.

barbecue sauce Combine ingredients in medium saucepan; bring to the boil. Cool 10 minutes.

red cabbage coleslaw Combine sour cream, juice and the water in screw-top jar; shake well. Combine dressing in large bowl with cabbage and onion. Cover; refrigerate until required.

preparation time *15 minutes (plus refrigeration time)*
cooking time *25 minutes* serves *4*
nutritional count per serving *39.9g total fat (15.2g saturated fat); 3210kJ (768 cal); 44.4g carbohydrate; 53.6g protein; 8g fibre*

pork neck with five-spice star-anise glaze

mixed grill with warm potato salad

pork neck with five-spice star-anise glaze

1kg piece pork neck
1 clove garlic, sliced thinly
4cm piece ginger (20g), sliced thinly
2 x 100g packets baby asian greens

five-spice star-anise glaze
1¼ cups (310ml) water
1 cup (220g) firmly packed brown sugar
3 fresh long red chillies, chopped finely
1 star anise
1 teaspoon five-spice powder
⅓ cup (80ml) light soy sauce
¼ cup (60ml) rice vinegar

1 Make five-spice star-anise glaze.

2 Make several shallow cuts in pork. Press garlic and ginger into cuts; brush ¼ cup of the glaze over pork. Reserve remaining glaze.

3 Cook pork in covered barbecue, using indirect heat, following manufacturer's instructions, 30 minutes. Turn pork; cook, covered, further 30 minutes. Increase heat to high; cook, uncovered, 5 minutes, turning and brushing constantly with remaining glaze. Remove pork from heat. Cover pork; stand 15 minutes then slice thickly.

4 Meanwhile, place reserved glaze in small saucepan; simmer about 5 minutes or until thickened slightly. Cool.

5 Combine asian greens with glaze in medium bowl; serve with pork.

five-spice star-anise glaze Combine the water and sugar in medium saucepan; simmer about 10 minutes or until glaze thickens slightly. Remove from heat; stir in remaining ingredients.

preparation time *15 minutes* (plus standing time)
cooking time *1 hour 20 minutes* serves 6
nutritional count per serving *13.4g total fat
(4.5g saturated fat); 1714kJ (410 cal);
36.4g carbohydrate; 36.5g protein; 0.6g fibre*

mixed grill with warm potato salad

700g kipfler potatoes, halved lengthways
1 tablespoon olive oil
2 cloves garlic, crushed
2 teaspoons caraway seeds
½ small cabbage (600g), shredded coarsely
4 x 100g pork butterflied steaks
4 thick pork sausages (480g)
4 thin bacon rashers (120g), rind removed
⅓ cup (80ml) olive oil, extra
¼ cup (60ml) white wine vinegar
2 teaspoons dijon mustard

1 Combine potato, oil, garlic and seeds in large lightly oiled shallow disposable baking dish. Cook potato in covered barbecue, using indirect heat, following manufacturer's instructions, 30 minutes or until potato is browned lightly.

2 Add cabbage to potato. Cook in covered barbecue, using indirect heat, about 15 minutes or until cabbage just wilts. Remove from heat; cover to keep warm.

3 Cook steaks, sausages and bacon on heated oiled barbecue until cooked through. Remove from heat; cover to keep warm.

4 Combine extra oil, vinegar and mustard in large bowl with potato mixture. Serve mixed grill with warm salad.

preparation time *25 minutes*
cooking time *45 minutes* serves 4
nutritional count per serving *61g total fat
(17.9g saturated fat); 2724kJ (891 cal);
31.2g carbohydrate; 49.7g protein; 10.1g fibre*

pork with salsa verde

800g pork fillets
2 cloves garlic, crushed
2 tablespoons olive oil
2 teaspoons finely grated lemon rind
2 teaspoons lemon juice

salsa verde
1 cup coarsely chopped fresh flat-leaf parsley
½ cup coarsely chopped fresh mint
2 tablespoons lemon juice
2 tablespoons rinsed, drained baby capers
1 clove garlic, crushed
¼ cup (60ml) olive oil

1   Make salsa verde.

2   Combine pork in large bowl with garlic, oil, rind and juice.

3   Cook pork on heated oiled barbecue until cooked through. Cover pork; stand 5 minutes then slice thinly. Serve pork with salsa verde.

salsa verde   Combine ingredients in small bowl.

preparation time *10 minutes*
cooking time *20 minutes* serves *4*
nutritional count per serving *27.6g total fat (4.8g saturated fat); 1814kJ (434 cal); 1.6g carbohydrate; 44.6g protein; 1.7g fibre*

harissa and lime-rubbed pork

½ cup (150g) harissa paste
2 teaspoons finely grated lime rind
1 tablespoon lime juice
1 clove garlic, crushed
800g pork fillets

1   Combine harissa, rind, juice, garlic and pork in large bowl.

2   Cook pork on heated oiled barbecue until browned all over. Cover pork; cook further 10 minutes or until cooked through. Stand pork 5 minutes then slice thickly.

preparation time *5 minutes*
cooking time *20 minutes* serves *4*
nutritional count per serving *16.3g total fat (2.8g saturated fat); 1463kJ (350 cal); 3g carbohydrate; 45.9g protein; 4˙g fibre*

pork with salsa verde

harissa and lime-rubbed pork

chilli pork burger

700g pork mince
1 small red onion (100g), chopped finely
⅓ cup coarsely chopped fresh coriander
¼ cup (15g) stale breadcrumbs
1 egg
1 fresh long red chilli, chopped finely
4 hamburger buns (360g)
⅓ cup (100g) mayonnaise
50g mizuna
⅓ cup (25g) fried shallots

caramelised capsicum salsa
1 medium red capsicum (200g), sliced thinly
1 large red onion (300g), sliced thinly
½ cup (125ml) sweet chilli sauce

1 Combine pork in large bowl with onion, coriander, breadcrumbs, egg and chilli; shape mixture into four patties.

2 Cook patties on heated oiled barbecue until cooked through.

3 Meanwhile, make caramelised capsicum salsa.

4 Split buns in half; toast on heated oiled barbecue. Spread mayonnaise on bun bases; sandwich mizuna, patties, salsa and shallots between bun halves.

caramelised capsicum salsa Cook capsicum and onion on heated oiled flat plate until onion softens. Add sauce; cook, stirring, about 2 minutes or until mixture caramelises.

preparation time *15 minutes*
cooking time *20 minutes* serves *4*
nutritional count per serving *26.6g total fat (6.6g saturated fat); 3018kJ (722 cal); 68.6g carbohydrate; 48.1g protein; 7.2g fibre*

Fried shallots can be purchased at all Asian grocery stores; once opened, they will keep for months if stored in a tightly sealed glass jar. Make your own by frying thinly sliced peeled shallots or baby onions until golden brown and crisp.

glazed pork and watercress salad

¼ cup (90g) honey
¼ cup (85g) tamarind concentrate
3cm piece fresh ginger (15g), grated
2 cloves garlic, crushed
800g pork fillets
100g watercress, trimmed
1 medium red onion (170g), sliced thinly
2 lebanese cucumbers (260g), seeded, sliced thinly
1 medium yellow capsicum (200g), sliced thinly
½ cup (75g) roasted unsalted cashews

1 Combine honey, tamarind, ginger and garlic in small jug. Combine pork with a third of the honey mixture in medium bowl.

2 Cook pork on heated oiled barbecue until cooked through. Cover pork; stand 10 minutes then slice thickly.

3 Meanwhile, combine remaining ingredients with half the remaining honey mixture in medium bowl.

4 Drizzle pork with remaining honey mixture; serve with salad.

preparation time *15 minutes*
cooking time *15 minutes* serves *4*
nutritional count per serving *14.1g total fat*
(3.2g saturated fat); 1885kJ (451 cal);
29.9g carbohydrate; 49.6g protein; 4.3g fibre

lemon chilli pork with italian brown rice salad

2 teaspoons finely grated lemon rind
2 tablespoons lemon juice
½ teaspoon dried chilli flakes
1 tablespoon olive oil
4 x 250g pork cutlets

italian brown rice salad
1 cup (200g) brown long-grain rice
1 medium red capsicum (200g), chopped finely
½ cup (60g) seeded black olives, chopped coarsely
2 tablespoons rinsed, drained capers
½ cup coarsely chopped fresh basil
⅓ cup coarsely chopped fresh flat-leaf parsley
2 tablespoons lemon juice
1 tablespoon olive oil

1 Combine rind, juice, chilli, oil and pork in medium bowl. Cover; refrigerate until required.

2 Make italian brown rice salad.

3 Cook pork on heated oiled barbecue until cooked through. Serve with rice salad.

italian brown rice salad Cook rice in large saucepan of boiling water, uncovered, until tender; drain. Rinse under cold water; drain. Combine rice in large bowl with remaining ingredients.

preparation time *35 minutes*
cooking time *50 minutes* serves *4*
nutritional count per serving *14.7g total fat*
(2.9g saturated fat); 1969kJ (471 cal);
46.4g carbohydrate; 35.7g protein; 3g fibre

glazed pork and watercress salad

lemon chilli pork with italian brown rice salad

best desserts
for barbecues

313

citrus salad with lime and mint granita, page 316

Choose sweet treats that can be cooked in advance and kept in the freezer or refrigerator, such as ice-blocks or a cheesecake. If you don't have time, some freshly cut fruit is a refreshing and light end to the day and can be eaten by hand without need for a plate.

citrus salad with lime and mint granita

2 medium oranges (480g)
2 small pink grapefruits (700g)
⅓ cup finely chopped fresh mint
2 tablespoons icing sugar
1 tablespoon lime juice
2 cups ice cubes

1 Segment oranges and grapefruits into medium bowl.

2 Blend or process mint, sifted icing sugar, juice and ice until ice is crushed; serve with fruit.

preparation time *15 minutes* serves *4*
nutritional count per serving *0.4g total fat*
(0g saturated fat); 385kJ (92 cal);
18.1g carbohydrate; 2.1g protein; 2.7g fibre

lime sorbet

2 tablespoons finely grated lime rind
1 cup (220g) caster sugar
2½ cups (625ml) water
¾ cup (180ml) lime juice
1 egg white

1 Stir rind, sugar and the water in medium saucepan over high heat until sugar dissolves; bring to the boil. Reduce heat; simmer, uncovered, without stirring, 5 minutes. Transfer to large heatproof jug, cool to room temperature; stir in juice.

2 Pour sorbet mixture into loaf pan; cover tightly with foil. Freeze 3 hours or overnight.

3 Process mixture with egg white until smooth. Return to loaf pan; cover, freeze until firm. Serve sprinkled with extra lime rind, if desired.

preparation time *20 minutes*
(plus cooling and freezing time)
cooking time *10 minutes* serves *8*
nutritional count per serving *0.1g total fat*
(0g saturated fat); 472kJ (113 cal);
27.9g carbohydrate; 0.7g protein; 0.2g fibre

variations

grapefruit sorbet Replace lime rind and lime juice with 2 tablespoons finely grated ruby grapefruit rind and ¾ cup (180ml) ruby red grapefruit juice. Follow recipe as per instructions. Serve sprinkled with extra grapefruit rind, if desired.

nutritional count per serving *0g total fat*
(0g saturated fat); 481kJ (115 cal);
29.3g carbohydrate; 0.6g protein; 0.1g fibre

blood orange sorbet Replace lime rind and lime juice with 2 tablespoons finely grated blood orange rind and 1 cup (250ml) blood orange juice. Follow recipe as per instructions. Serve sprinkled with extra blood orange rind, if desired.

nutritional count per serving *0g total fat*
(0g saturated fat); 497kJ (119 cal);
30.2g carbohydrate; 0.6g protein; 0.1g fibre

top to bottom: lime sorbet; grapefruit sorbet; blood orange sorbet

pineapple and mint ice-blocks

lemonade ice-blocks

orange and mango ice-blocks

raspberry ice-blocks

pineapple and mint ice-blocks

1½ cups (375ml) pineapple juice
2 tablespoons icing sugar
2 teaspoons finely chopped fresh mint

1 Combine juice, sifted icing sugar and mint in medium jug.

2 Pour mixture into six ¼-cup ice-block moulds. Press lids on firmly; freeze overnight.

preparation time 5 minutes
(plus freezing time) makes 6
nutritional count per ice-block 0.1g total fat
(0g saturated fat); 188kJ (45 cal);
10.6g carbohydrate; 0.2g protein; 0g fibre

lemonade ice-blocks

¼ cup (60ml) lemon juice
⅔ cup (110g) icing sugar
1 cup (250ml) sparkling mineral water

1 Stir juice and sifted icing sugar in medium jug until sugar dissolves. Stir in mineral water.

2 Pour mixture into six ¼-cup ice-block moulds. Press lids on firmly; freeze overnight.

preparation time 5 minutes
(plus freezing time) makes 6
nutritional count per ice-block 0g total fat
(0g saturated fat); 318kJ (76 cal);
18.5g carbohydrate; 0.1g protein; 0g fibre

orange and mango ice-blocks

425g can sliced mango in natural juice
½ cup (125ml) orange juice

1 Strain mango over small bowl; reserve ¼ cup juice.

2 Blend or process mango slices, reserved juice and orange juice until smooth.

3 Pour mixture into six ¼-cup ice-block moulds. Press lids on firmly; freeze overnight.

preparation time 5 minutes
(plus freezing time) makes 6
nutritional count per ice-block 0.1g total fat
(0g saturated fat); 196kJ (47 cal);
10.3g carbohydrate; 0.7g protein; 0.7g fibre

raspberry ice-blocks

1 cup (150g) frozen raspberries
⅓ cup (55g) icing sugar
1 cup (250ml) sparkling mineral water

1 Heat raspberries and sifted icing sugar in small saucepan over low heat, stirring occasionally, about 5 minutes
or until raspberries soften. Using back of large spoon, push raspberry mixture through sieve into medium jug; discard seeds, cool.

2 Stir mineral water into jug. Pour mixture into six ¼-cup ice-block moulds. Press lids on firmly; freeze overnight.

preparation time 10 minutes
(plus cooling and freezing time)
cooking time 5 minutes makes 6
nutritional count per ice-block 0.1g total fat
(0g saturated fat); 201kJ (48 cal);
10.6g carbohydrate; 0.3g protein; 1.4g fibre

black forest trifle

425g can seeded black cherries in syrup
350g un-iced chocolate cake
¼ cup (60ml) cherry brandy
2 teaspoons cocoa powder

chocolate custard
5 egg yolks
½ cup (110g) caster sugar
1 cup (250ml) milk
¾ cup (180ml) cream
100g dark eating chocolate, chopped coarsely

mascarpone cream
300ml cream
1 cup (250g) mascarpone cheese
2 teaspoons vanilla extract
¼ cup (40g) icing sugar

chocolate curls
100g dark chocolate Melts

1 Make chocolate custard. Make mascarpone cream.

2 Drain cherries; reserve ¼ cup of the syrup.

3 Coarsely chop cake, place in deep 3-litre (12-cup) serving bowl; sprinkle with cherries and combined brandy and reserved syrup. Top with chocolate custard then mascarpone cream. Cover trifle; refrigerate 3 hours or overnight.

4 Make chocolate curls. Top trifle with chocolate curls and sifted cocoa powder.

chocolate custard Whisk egg yolks and sugar in medium bowl until combined. Combine milk, cream and chocolate in medium saucepan; stir over low heat until mixture comes to the boil, remove from heat. Gradually whisk hot chocolate mixture into yolk mixture. Return mixture to pan; stir over low heat, without boiling, about 10 minutes or until mixture is slightly thickened and coats the back of a spoon. Cover; refrigerate until chilled.

mascarpone cream Beat ingredients in small bowl with electric mixer until soft peaks form. Cover; refrigerate until chilled.

chocolate curls Place chocolate in small heatproof bowl; using wooden spoon, stir chocolate over small saucepan of simmering water until smooth. Spread chocolate evenly over marble or foil-covered surface. When chocolate is almost set, drag ice-cream scoop over surface of chocolate to make curls.

preparation time *35 minutes (plus refrigeration time)*
cooking time *15 minutes* serves *10*
nutritional count per serving *49.5g total fat
(30.6g saturated fat); 2855kJ (683 cal);
52g carbohydrate; 7.9g protein; 1.1g fibre*

The chocolate custard can be made a day ahead. Keep, covered, in the refrigerator.

banana caramel sundae

mango and passionfruit tiramisu

best desserts for barbecues

banana caramel sundae

70g dark eating chocolate, chopped finely
⅔ cup (70g) roasted walnuts, chopped coarsely
1 litre vanilla ice-cream
4 medium bananas (800g), chopped coarsely

caramel sauce
100g butter
½ cup (125ml) cream
½ cup (110g) firmly packed brown sugar

1 Make caramel sauce.

2 Divide one third of the sauce among six ¾ cup (180ml) glasses; divide half the chocolate, half the nuts, half the ice-cream and half the banana among glasses. Repeat layering process; top with sauce.

caramel sauce Combine ingredients in small saucepan. Stir over low heat until sugar dissolves; bring to the boil. Reduce heat; simmer, uncovered, 5 minutes. Cool.

preparation time *10 minutes (plus cooling time)*
cooking time *10 minutes* serves *6*
nutritional count per serving *41.7g total fat
(22.4g saturated fat); 2579kJ (617 cal);
56.1g carbohydrate; 6.9g protein; 2.4g fibre*

mango and passionfruit tiramisu

1 cup (250ml) passionfruit pulp
1¾ cups (430ml) thickened cream
¼ cup (40g) icing sugar
1 teaspoon finely grated lime rind
1 cup (250g) mascarpone cheese
½ cup (125ml) coconut-flavoured liqueur
4 medium mangoes (1.7kg), chopped coarsely
1 cup (250ml) pineapple juice
250g sponge finger biscuits

1 Strain passionfruit pulp over small bowl; reserve seeds and juice separately.

2 Beat cream, sifted icing sugar and rind in small bowl with electric mixer until soft peaks form. Transfer to medium bowl; fold in mascarpone and 2 teaspoons of the liqueur.

3 Combine mango, passionfruit seeds and 2 teaspoons of the remaining liqueur in medium bowl.

4 Combine pineapple juice, passionfruit juice and remaining liqueur in medium bowl.

5 Soak half the sponge fingers, one at a time, in pineapple juice mixture. Arrange soaked sponge fingers over base of shallow 2.5-litre (10-cup) serving dish. Top with half the mascarpone mixture; sprinkle with half the mango mixture. Repeat with remaining sponge fingers, pineapple mixture, mascarpone mixture and mango mixture. Cover; refrigerate 6 hours or overnight.

preparation time *30 minutes
(plus refrigeration time)* serves *8*
nutritional count per serving *36.5g total fat
(23.6g saturated fat); 2516kJ (602 cal);
56.6g carbohydrate; 7.7g protein; 7g fibre*

You need at least 12 passionfruit to get the amount of passionfruit pulp needed for this recipe. We used Malibu in this recipe, but you can use any coconut-flavoured liqueur you like.

summer berry and almond tart

1⅔ cups (250g) plain flour
⅓ cup (55g) icing sugar
2 teaspoons grated orange rind
150g cold butter, chopped coarsely
1 egg
350g fresh mixed berries

almond filling
90g butter
1 teaspoon vanilla extract
½ cup (110g) caster sugar
1 egg
1 tablespoon plain flour
1 cup (100g) almond meal

1 Process sifted flour and icing sugar, rind and butter until combined. Add egg; process until pastry just comes together. Shape pastry into round. Cover with plastic wrap; refrigerate 1 hour.

2 Roll pastry between two sheets of baking paper until large enough to line base and side of 26cm-round loose-based flan tin. Ease pastry into tin, pressing lightly into side. Trim edge with sharp knife or rolling pin. Place tin on oven tray; refrigerate 15 minutes.

3 Preheat oven to 180°C/160°C fan-forced.

4 Cover pastry with baking paper, fill with dried beans or rice; bake 10 minutes. Remove paper and beans; bake further 5 minutes or until pastry is golden brown. Cool.

5 Meanwhile, make almond filling.

6 Spoon filling into pastry base; scatter berries over filling. Bake 35 minutes or until filling is golden and firm; cool.

7 Serve with whipped cream and dusted with sifted icing sugar, if you like.

almond filling Beat butter, extract and sugar in small bowl with electric mixer until pale. Beat in egg until combined; stir in flour and almond meal.

preparation time *30 minutes (plus refrigeration time)*
cooking time *50 minutes* serves *8*
nutritional count per serving *33.3g total fat (17.1g saturated fat); 2190kJ (524 cal); 46.4g carbohydrate; 8.6g protein; 3.4g fibre*

This recipe can be made a day ahead. The pastry is suitable to freeze.

poached nectarines with orange almond bread

3 cups (750g) water
1 cup (220g) caster sugar
1 star anise
10cm strip orange rind
8 small nectarines (800g)
⅔ cup (190g) yogurt

orange almond bread
2 egg whites
⅓ cup (75g) caster sugar
¾ cup (110g) plain flour
1 teaspoon finely grated orange rind
¾ cup (120g) blanched almonds

1 Make orange almond bread.

2 Combine the water, sugar, star anise and rind in medium saucepan; stir over medium heat until sugar dissolves. Bring to the boil; boil, uncovered, 2 minutes. Add nectarines, reduce heat; simmer, uncovered, 20 minutes. Cool nectarines 10 minutes in poaching liquid.

3 Using slotted spoon, transfer nectarines to serving dishes; bring liquid in pan to the boil. Boil, uncovered, about 5 minutes or until syrup reduces to 1 cup, strain into small bowl.

4 Cool syrup to room temperature. Pour ¼ cup of the syrup over nectarines; serve with yogurt and almond bread.

orange almond bread Preheat oven to 180°C/160°C fan-forced. Grease and line 8cm x 25cm bar cake pan. Beat egg whites in small bowl with electric mixer until soft peaks form. Gradually add sugar, 1 tablespoon at a time, beating until sugar dissolves between additions; transfer to medium bowl. Gently fold in sifted flour, rind and nuts; spread into prepared pan. Bake, uncovered, about 30 minutes or until browned lightly; cool in pan. Wrap in foil; refrigerate 3 hours or overnight. Preheat oven to 150°C/130°C fan-forced. Using serrated knife, cut bread into 3mm slices; place slices on baking-paper-lined oven trays. Bake, uncovered, about 15 minutes or until crisp.

preparation time *25 minutes*
(plus cooling and refrigeration time)
cooking time *1 hour 20 minutes* serves 4
nutritional count per serving *20.6g total fat*
(3.3g saturated fat); 2867kJ (686 cal);
112.6g carbohydrate; 15.5g protein; 7.9g fibre

baked vanilla cheesecake with poached pears and apricots

250g plain sweet biscuits
125g butter, melted
3 x 250g packets cream cheese, softened
¾ cup (165g) caster sugar
2 tablespoons vanilla extract
½ teaspoon grated lemon rind
2 tablespoons lemon juice
4 eggs, separated
¾ cup (180ml) cream

poached pears and apricots
2 cups (500ml) water
1 cup (250ml) orange juice
¼ cup (55g) sugar
1 cup (150g) dried apricots
5 small pears (900g), peeled, halved, cored
1 cinnamon stick
¼ teaspoon ground nutmeg
2 tablespoons orange-flavoured liqueur

1 Process biscuits until mixture resembles fine breadcrumbs. Add butter; process until just combined.

2 Press crumb mixture evenly over base and side of 23cm springform tin. Cover; refrigerate 30 minutes or until firm.

3 Meanwhile, preheat oven to 160°C/140°C fan-forced.

4 Beat cream cheese, sugar and extract in large bowl with electric mixer until smooth. Add rind, juice, egg yolks and cream; beat until light and fluffy.

5 Beat two of the egg whites in small bowl with electric mixer until firm peaks form; fold into cream cheese mixture. Discard remaining egg whites.

6 Place tin on oven tray; pour cheesecake mixture into base. Bake about 1 hour or until just firm. Cool in oven with door ajar.

7 Cover cheesecake; refrigerate 3 hours or overnight.

8 Make poached pears and apricots.

9 Remove cheesecake from tin just before serving; serve with poached fruit.

poached pears and apricots Combine ingredients in large saucepan; simmer, covered, about 10 minutes or until pears are just tender. Discard cinnamon stick; strain fruit mixture over large heatproof bowl. Return liquid to pan; boil, uncovered, about 10 minutes or until reduced to 1 cup. Add syrup to fruit in bowl; cool.

preparation time *35 minutes*
(plus refrigeration and cooling time)
cooking time *1 hour 20 minutes* serves *10*
nutritional count per serving *49.1g total fat
(30.4g saturated fat); 3194kJ (764 cal);
61.8g carbohydrate; 12.1g protein; 3.2g fibre*

We used Cointreau in this recipe, but you can use any orange-flavoured liqueur you like. You need 2 egg whites only for this recipe, so keep them separate when separating eggs. Discard remaining 2 egg whites, or keep for another use.

pineapple and kiwifruit salad in basil lemon syrup

1½ cups (375ml) water
2 x 5cm strips lemon rind
½ cup (125ml) lemon juice
1 tablespoon caster sugar
¼ cup firmly packed fresh basil leaves
1 small pineapple (900g), quartered, sliced thinly
6 medium kiwifruit (510g), sliced thinly
⅓ cup (80ml) passionfruit pulp
1 tablespoon finely shredded fresh basil

1 Combine the water, rind, juice, sugar and basil leaves in medium frying pan; bring to the boil. Reduce heat; simmer, uncovered, 20 minutes. Strain syrup into medium jug; discard rind and basil. Cool 10 minutes; refrigerate until required.

2 Just before serving, combine syrup in large bowl with remaining ingredients.

preparation time *20 minutes (plus refrigeration time)*
cooking time *20 minutes* serves *4*
nutritional count per serving *0.5g total fat
(0g saturated fat); 627kJ (150 cal);
26.6g carbohydrate; 3.6g protein; 9g fibre*

You need at least four passionfruit to get the amount of passionfruit pulp needed for this recipe.

frozen mango parfait

1 medium mango (430g), chopped coarsely
2 cups (440g) low-fat ricotta cheese
¾ cup (165g) caster sugar
300ml light thickened cream

tropical fruit salsa
¼ cup (55g) caster sugar
¼ cup (60ml) water
2 medium kiwifruit (170g), chopped coarsely
1 medium mango (430g), chopped coarsely
2 kaffir lime leaves, sliced thinly

1 Line base of 14cm x 21cm loaf pan with foil, extending 5cm over long edges.

2 Blend or process mango until smooth.

3 Beat cheese and sugar in small bowl with electric mixer until smooth; transfer mixture to large bowl. Beat cream in small bowl with electric mixer until soft peaks form; fold cream into ricotta mixture.

4 Drop alternate spoonfuls of cheese mixture and mango pulp into pan. Pull skewer backwards and forwards through parfait mixture several times for marbled effect; smooth surface with spatula. Cover with foil; freeze overnight.

5 Make tropical fruit salsa 1 hour before serving. Cover, refrigerate until cold. Serve parfait topped with salsa.

tropical fruit salsa Combine sugar and the water in small saucepan; bring to the boil. Reduce heat; simmer, uncovered, without stirring, 5 minutes; cool. Combine sugar syrup with remaining ingredients in medium bowl.

preparation time *20 minutes (plus freezing time)*
cooking time *10 minutes* serves *12*
nutritional count per serving *12.3g total fat
(8g saturated fat); 986kJ (236 cal);
27.4g carbohydrate; 4.7g protein; 1.2g fibre*

pineapple and kiwifruit salad in basil lemon syrup

frozen mango parfait

The brownie and the sauce can be made up to two days ahead. Store brownie in an airtight container; store sauce, covered, in the refrigerator. Reheat both brownie and sauce before serving with ice-cream.

We used Frangelico in this recipe, but you can use any hazelnut-flavoured liqueur you like. Tia Maria, or similar coffee-flavoured liqueurs, also go well in this dessert.

brownies with chocolate sauce

150g butter, chopped coarsely
300g dark eating chocolate, chopped coarsely
1½ cups (330g) firmly packed brown sugar
4 eggs, beaten lightly
1 cup (150g) plain flour
½ cup (120g) sour cream
½ cup (60g) hazelnuts, roasted, chopped coarsely
vanilla ice-cream, to serve

warm chocolate sauce
150g dark eating chocolate, chopped coarsely
1 cup (250ml) cream
⅓ cup (75g) firmly packed brown sugar
2 teaspoons hazelnut-flavoured liqueur

1 Preheat oven to 180°C/160°C fan-forced. Line base and sides of 20cm x 30cm lamington pan with baking paper.

2 Combine butter and chocolate in medium saucepan; stir over low heat until chocolate is just melted. Transfer chocolate mixture to medium bowl; stir in sugar and egg then sifted flour, sour cream and nuts. Spread mixture into prepared pan. Bake about 30 minutes.

3 Meanwhile, make warm chocolate sauce.

4 Cut warm brownie into 16 pieces. Serve brownies with ice-cream and drizzled with warm chocolate sauce.

warm chocolate sauce Combine chocolate, cream and sugar in small saucepan; stir over low heat until mixture is smooth. Simmer, uncovered, 1 minute. Remove from heat; stir in liqueur.

preparation time *15 minutes (plus cooling time)*
cooking time *40 minutes* serves *8*
nutritional count per serving *58.3g total fat (33.6g saturated fat), 4059kJ (971 cal); 100.1g carbohydrate; 10.5g protein; 2.2g fibre*

glossary

Allspice also known as pimento or jamaican pepper; so-named because it tastes like a combination of nutmeg, cumin, clove and cinnamon. Available whole or ground.

Aromatic bitters a mixture of herbs and citrus dissolved in alcohol with a bitter or bittersweet flavour.

Artichoke heart tender centre of the globe artichoke; harvested from the plant after the prickly choke is removed. Buy from delicatessens or canned in brine.

Baba ghanoush a roasted eggplant (aubergine) dip or spread.

Bacon
rashers also known as bacon slices; made from cured and smoked pork side.
shortcut a "half rasher"; the streaky (belly), narrow portion of the rasher has been removed leaving the choice cut eye meat (large end).
streaky is the fatty end of a bacon rasher without the lean (eye) meat.

Banana leaves foil can be used if banana leaves are unavailable. Order from fruit and vegetable stores. Cut with a sharp knife close to the main stem, then immerse briefly in hot water so leaves will be pliable.

Basil there are many types, but the most commonly used basil in cooking is sweet, or common, basil.

thai also known as horapa; has smallish leaves and a sweet licorice/aniseed taste. Available from Asian grocery stores, major supermarkets and greengrocers.

Beans
broad also known as fava, windsor and horse beans; available dried, fresh, canned and frozen. Fresh and frozen forms should be peeled twice (discarding both the outer long green pod and the beige-green tough inner shell).
dried black also known as turtle beans or black kidney beans; an earthy-flavoured dried bean completely different from the better-known chinese black beans (which are fermented soya beans).
four-bean mix consists of kidney beans, butter beans, chickpeas and cannellini beans.
green also known as french or string beans; this long thin fresh bean is consumed in its entirety once cooked.
kidney medium-sized red bean, slightly floury in texture yet sweet in flavour; sold dried or canned.
sprouts also known as bean shoots; tender new shoots of assorted beans and seeds germinated for consumption as sprouts (including mung beans, soya beans, alfalfa and snow pea sprouts).
white in this book, some recipes may simply call for "white beans", a generic term we use for canned or dried cannellini, haricot, navy or great northern beans.

Beef
calves liver tender with a fine texture and delicious taste; has a better flavour than beef liver.
eye-fillet tenderloin fillet; an expensive cut of meat with a fine texture.
fillet a generic name given to a steak cut from the tenderloin.
minute very thin boneless beef, usually scored and pounded to tenderise it.
new-york cut boneless striploin steak.
rump boneless tender cut taken from the hindquarter.
scotch fillet cut from the muscle running behind the shoulder along the spine. Also known as cube roll; cuts include standing rib roast and rib-eye.
sirloin cut from the lower portion of the ribs, continuing off the tenderloin, from which filet mignon is cut.
skirt steak lean, flavourful coarse-grained cut.
t-bone sirloin steak with the bone in and eye fillet attached.

Beetroot also known as red beets or beets; a firm, round root vegetable.

Betel leaves from the betel plant; sold in bunches in Asian grocery stores. Most often used as a wrapping for spiced minced meat and other snacks. The leaves can also be used as a herb in Asian cooking.

Bicarbonate of soda also known as baking or carb soda; a mild alkali used as a leavening agent in baking.

Biscuits, plain sweet also known as cookies; a crisp sweet biscuit without icing or any fillings.

Blood orange a virtually seedless citrus fruit with blood-red flesh; it has a sweet, non-acidic pulp and juice, with slight strawberry or raspberry overtones.

Breads
ciabatta in Italian, the word means slipper, which is the traditional shape of this popular white bread with a crisp crust.
flat breads also known as roti, chapatti, phulka and parantha. Made of wheat and water and used for scooping or wrapping.
focaccia a popular Italian flat, yeast bread. The top is dimpled and brushed with oil to keep the bread moist and flavourful. The most basic focaccia is simply a herbed and oiled bread with salt, but the variations are endless.
french stick also known as french bread, french loaf or baguette; formed into a long, narrow cylindrical loaf with a crisp brown crust and light chewy interior. A standard french stick is 5-6cm wide and 3-4cm tall, but can be up to a meter in length.
lavash flat, unleavened bread of Mediterranean origin.
pitta also known as lebanese bread. This wheat-flour pocket bread is sold in large, flat pieces that separate into two thin rounds. Also available in small pieces called pocket pitta.

sourdough so-named, not because it's sour in taste, but because it's made by using a small amount of "starter dough", which contains a yeast culture, mixed into flour and water. Part of the resulting dough is then saved to use as the starter dough next time.

tortilla thin, round, unleavened bread originating in Mexico. Two kinds are available, one made from wheat flour and the other from corn.

turkish also known as pide; comes in long (about 45cm) flat loaves as well as individual rounds. Made from wheat flour and sprinkled with sesame seeds or kalonji (black onion seeds).

Breadcrumbs
fresh bread, usually white, processed into crumbs.

packaged prepared fine-textured, but crunchy, white breadcrumbs.

stale made by processing one- or two-day-old bread.

Broccolini a cross between broccoli and chinese kale; has long asparagus-like stems with a long loose floret, both completely edible. Resembles broccoli in look but is milder and sweeter in taste.

Buk choy also known as bok choy, pak choi, chinese white cabbage or chinese chard; has a fresh, mild mustard taste. Baby buk choy, also known as pak kat farang or shanghai bok choy, is much smaller and more tender than buk choy.

Burghul also known as bulghur or bulgar wheat; hulled steamed wheat kernels that, once dried, are crushed into various size grains. Not the same as cracked wheat. Found in most supermarkets or health food stores.

Butter use salted or unsalted (sweet) butter; 125g is equal to one stick (4 ounces) of butter.

Buttermilk originally the term given to the slightly sour liquid left after butter was churned from cream, today it is made similarly to yogurt. Found in the refrigerated section in supermarkets. Despite its name, it is low in fat.

Caperberries fruit formed after the caper buds have flowered; caperberries are pickled, usually with their stalks intact.

Capers the grey-green buds of a warm climate shrub (usually Mediterranean); sold either dried and salted, or pickled in a vinegar brine. Baby capers are smaller, fuller-flavoured and more expensive than the full-sized ones. Capers should be rinsed well before using.

Capsicum also known as bell pepper or, simply, pepper. Come in many colours: red, green, yellow, orange and purplish-black. Discard seeds and membranes before use.

Caraway seeds have a sweetly rich flavour; available in seed or ground form.

Cardamom has a distinctive, aromatic, sweetly rich flavour; is one of the world's most expensive spices. Available in pod, seed or ground form.

Champagne, brut a dry unsweetened Champagne.

Cheese
bocconcini from "boccone", meaning mouthful in Italian; a walnut-sized baby mozzarella. Is a delicate, semi-soft, white cheese. Sold fresh, it spoils rapidly so will only keep for one or two days refrigerated in brine.

brie often referred to in France as the queen of cheeses; soft-ripened cow-milk cheese with a delicate, creamy texture and a rich, sweet taste that varies from buttery to mushroomy.

camembert made from cows' milk. Has a creamy yellow flesh encased in a speckled, floury, mouldy-looking crust. A ripe camembert is six weeks old with a fruity, tangy fragrance.

cheddar the most common cows-milk tasty cheese; should be aged, hard and have a pronounced bite.

cream commonly known as Philadelphia or Philly; a soft cows-milk cheese. Also available as spreadable light cream cheese, which is a blend of cottage and cream cheeses.

fetta a crumbly textured goat- or sheep-milk cheese having a sharp, salty taste. Ripened and stored in salted whey.

fontina a smooth, firm cows-milk cheese with a creamy, nutty taste and brown or red rind.

goats made from goats milk; has an earthy, strong taste. Available in soft, crumbly and firm textures, in various shapes and sizes, and sometimes rolled in ash or herbs.

haloumi has a semi-firm, spongy texture and very salty yet sweet flavour. Ripened and stored in salted whey, it holds its shape well when heated. Best eaten while still warm as it becomes rubbery when cool.

mascarpone an ivory-coloured, buttery-rich, cream-like cheese made from cows' milk; most often used in desserts.

mozzarella soft, spun-curd cheese; most popular pizza cheese because of its low melting point and elasticity when heated.

parmesan also known as parmigiana; a hard, grainy cows-milk cheese.

pecorino the generic name for cheeses made from sheep milk. Is a hard, white to pale yellow cheese; if you can't find it, use parmesan.

ricotta a soft, white, sweet, cows-milk cheese having a slightly grainy texture. The name roughly translates as "cooked again" and refers to ricotta's manufacture from a whey that is itself a by-product of other cheese making.

Cherry brandy also known as kirsch, which is short for kirschwasser, and literally translates as cherry water. Has a robust flavour without a hint of sweetness. This sets kirsch apart from cherry liqueur, which is usually very sweet.

Chervil also known as cicily; mildly fennel-flavoured herb with curly dark-green leaves.

Chickpeas also called channa, garbanzos or hummus; an irregularly round, sandy-coloured legume.

Chilli always use rubber gloves when seeding and chopping fresh chillies as they can burn your skin. We use unseeded chillies in our recipes because the seeds contain the heat; use fewer chillies rather than seeding the lot.
banana also known as wax chillies or hungarian peppers; are almost as mild as capsicum but have a distinctively sweet sharpness to their taste. Sold in varying degrees of ripeness, they can be found in yellow, pale-green and red varieties at greengrocers and most major supermarkets.
cayenne pepper extremely hot, long, thin-fleshed, dried red chilli, usually purchased ground; both arbol and guajillo chillies are the fresh sources for cayenne.
chipotle (cheh-pote-lay) the name used for jalapeño chillies once they've been dried and smoked. Has a deep, intensely smoky flavour, rather than a searing heat; are dark brown, almost black in colour and wrinkled in appearance.
flakes also sold as crushed chilli; dehydrated deep-red extremely fine slices and whole seeds.
green any unripened chilli; also some particular varieties that are ripe when green, such as jalapeño, habanero, poblano or serrano.
jalapeño fairly hot green chilli, available in brine, bottled, or fresh from greengrocers.
long red available both fresh and dried; a generic term used for any moderately hot, long, thin chilli (6-8cm long).

pasilla (pah-see-yah) also known as "chile negro" because of its almost black skin; pungent, medium-hot, smoky, dried chilli measuring about 15cm to 20cm in length. Use sparingly until you discover the right amount for your palate.
pickled green green chillies available pickled in vinegar and sugar; from Asian grocery stores and some delicatessens.
powder the Asian variety is the hottest, made from dried ground thai red chillies; can be used instead of fresh chillies in the proportion of ½ teaspoon chilli powder to 1 medium chopped fresh red chilli.
red thai also known as "scuds"; tiny, hot and bright red in colour.

Chinese cooking wine also known as chinese rice wine or shao hsing; made from fermented rice, wheat, sugar and salt. Inexpensive and found in Asian grocery stores; if you can't find it, use mirin or sherry, instead.

Chives related to the onion and leek; has a subtle onion flavour.

Chocolate
choc Melts compounded dark chocolate discs ideal for melting and moulding.
dark eating made of cocoa liquor, cocoa butter and sugar.

Cinnamon dried inner bark of the shoots of the cinnamon tree; available in stick (quill) or ground form.

Cocoa powder also known as unsweetened cocoa; fermented, roasted cocoa beans that have been ground into a powder.

Coconut
cream obtained from the first pressing of the coconut flesh alone, without the addition of water; the second pressing (less rich) is sold as the milk. Available in cans and cartons at supermarkets.

flaked dried and flaked flesh of the coconut.
fresh to open a fresh coconut, pierce one of the eyes then roast briefly in a very hot oven only until cracks appear in the shell. Cool then break the coconut apart and grate or flake the firm white flesh.

Coriander also known as pak chee, cilantro or chinese parsley; bright-green leafy herb with a pungent flavour. Both the stems and roots of coriander are used; wash well before using. Coriander seeds are also available but are no substitute for fresh coriander, as the taste is very different.

Corn chips a crunchy corn snack. The corn is washed, then ground to produce a dough, which is rolled into a thin sheet and cut into various shapes. The dough is then toasted and fried until crisp.

Couscous a fine, grain-like cereal product made from semolina. A semolina flour and water dough is sieved then dehydrated to produce minuscule even-sized pellets of couscous; it is rehydrated by steaming, or with the addition of a warm liquid, and swells to three or four times its original size.

Cranberries, dried have the same slightly sour, succulent flavour as fresh cranberries. Available in supermarkets and health-food stores.

Cream we used fresh cream, unless otherwise stated. Also known as pure cream and pouring cream.
crème fraîche fermented cream with a tangy, nutty flavour and velvety texture.
sour a thick commercially-cultured soured cream. Light sour cream is also available.
thickened a whipping cream containing a thickener.

Cumin also known as zeera or comino; has a spicy, nutty flavour. Available in seed, dried and ground forms.

Currants, dried tiny, almost black raisins so-named after a grape variety that originated in Corinth, Greece.

Curry pastes
balti a medium-hot, aromatic paste containing coriander, fenugreek and mint, which gives it its distinctive mild "green" flavour.
green the hottest of the traditional pastes containing green chilli, garlic, shallot, lemon grass, salt, galangal, shrimp paste, kaffir lime peel, coriander seed, pepper, cumin and turmeric.
rogan josh a paste of medium heat, made from fresh chillies or paprika, tomato and spices, especially cardamom.
tandoori paste consisting of garlic, tamarind, ginger, chilli, coriander and various spices.

Daikon also known as giant white radish; has a sweet, fresh flavour without the bite of the common red radish. Used raw or cooked.

Dates fruit of the date palm tree, eaten fresh or dried. About 4-6cm in length, oval and plump and thin-skinned, with a honey-sweet flavour and a sticky texture.

Dill also known as dill weed; used fresh or dried, in seed form or ground. Has an anise/celery sweetness; its distinctive feathery, frond-like fresh leaves are grassier and more subtle than the dried version or the seeds.

Dukkah an Egyptian specialty made from various roasted nuts and spices. Dip bread into olive oil and then dip it into the dukkah for a tasty snack.

Eggplant also known as aubergine. Ranges in size from tiny to large, and in colour from pale-green to deep-purple. Also available char-grilled, packed in oil, in jars. Baby eggplant, also known as japanese or finger eggplant, are small and slender.

Fennel also known as finocchio or anise; a white to very pale green-white, firm, crisp, roundish vegetable about 8-12cm in diameter. The bulb has a slightly sweet, anise flavour but the leaves have a much stronger taste. Also the name given to dried seeds having a licorice flavour.

Figs vary in skin and flesh colour according to type, not ripeness. When ripe, should be unblemished and bursting with flesh; nectar beads at the base indicate when it's at its best.

Five-spice powder a fragrant mixture of cinnamon, cloves, star anise, sichuan pepper and fennel seeds. Also known as chinese five-spice.

Flour
plain an all-purpose flour, made from wheat.
self-raising plain flour sifted with baking powder in the proportion of 1 cup flour to 2 teaspoons baking powder.

Gai lan also known chinese broccoli, gai larn, kanah, gai lum and chinese kale; appreciated more for its stems than its coarse leaves.

Ginger, fresh also known as green or root ginger; the thick gnarled root of a tropical plant.

Gnocchi Italian "dumplings" made from potatoes, semolina or flour.

Golden syrup a by-product of refined sugarcane; pure maple syrup or honey can be substituted.

Guava nectar a liquid flavoured by the pulp from the tropical fruit guava. Has a tangy flavour that has a naturally rich sweetness. Available from some health-food stores.

Harissa paste a Moroccan sauce or paste made from dried chillies, cumin, garlic, oil and caraway seeds. It is available in supermarkets and Middle-Eastern grocery stores.

Honeydew a heavy oval fruit with a pale-green to yellow skin, delicate taste and pale green flesh.

Horseradish there are two commercially prepared horseradish products on the market – cream and prepared. These cannot be substituted one for the other in cooking but both can be used as table condiments.
cream a creamy paste that consists of grated horseradish, vinegar, oil and sugar.
prepared the preserved grated root.

Hummus a Middle Eastern salad or dip made from garlic, chickpeas, lemon juice and tahini (sesame seed paste); available from supermarkets.

Kaffir lime leaves also known as bai magrood; sold fresh, dried or frozen. Looks like two glossy dark green leaves joined end to end, forming a rounded hourglass shape. Dried leaves are less potent, so double the number called for in a recipe if you substitute them for fresh. A strip of fresh lime peel may be substituted for each kaffir lime leaf.

Kecap manis *see sauces.*

Kiwifruit also known as chinese gooseberry. Has a brown, somewhat hairy skin and bright-green or gold flesh with a sweet-tart flavour.

Kumara Polynesian name of orange-fleshed sweet potato often confused with yam.

Lamb
backstrap also known as eye of loin; the larger fillet from a row of loin chops or cutlets.
boned rolled loin loin that has had the bone removed.
chump cut from just above the hind legs to the mid-loin section; used for roasting or cut into chops.
cutlet small, tender rib chop.
diced cubed lean meat.
fillet extremely expensive, fine textured and very tender piece of tenderloin.
leg cut from the hindquarter.
loin chop cut from the back of the lamb; a tender, but expensive, cut.

Lebanese cucumber short, slender and thin-skinned. Probably the most popular variety because of its tender, edible skin, tiny, yielding seeds and sweet, fresh taste.

Leek a member of the onion family; looks like a large green onion but is more subtle and mild in flavour. Wash well before use. Pencil leeks, young, slender leeks, can be cooked and eaten like asparagus.

Lemon grass a tall, clumping, lemon-smelling and -tasting, sharp-edged grass; the white part of each stem is chopped and used in Asian cooking.

Lemon pepper also known as lemon pepper seasoning; a blend of crushed black pepper, lemon, herbs and spices.

Lemon thyme a herb with a lemony scent, which is due to the high level of citral in its leaves – an oil also found in lemon, orange, verbena and lemon grass. The citrus scent is enhanced by crushing the leaves in your hands before using the herb.

Lentils (red, brown, yellow) dried pulses often identified by, and named after, their colour.

Lettuce and salad greens
asian greens a mix of baby buk choy, choy sum, gai lan and water spinach. Store in the refrigerator and use within 1-2 days of buying.
butter small, round, loosely formed heads with a sweet flavour; soft, buttery-textured leaves range from pale green on the outer leaves to pale yellow-green inner leaves.
cos also known as romaine lettuce; the traditional caesar salad lettuce. Long, with leaves ranging from dark green on the outside to almost white near the core; the leaves have a stiff centre rib that gives a slight cupping effect to the leaf on either side.
curly endive also known as frisée, a curly-leafed green vegetable; used in salads.
iceberg a heavy, firm lettuce with tightly packed leaves and a crisp texture; the most common "family" lettuce used on sandwiches and in salads.
mesclun also known as salad mix or gourmet salad mix; a mixture of assorted young lettuce and other green leaves, including baby spinach leaves, mizuna and curly endive.
mizuna a wispy, feathered mild-tasting green salad leaf.
oak leaf also known as feuille de chene; curly-leafed but not as frizzy as the coral lettuce. Found in both red and green varieties.
radicchio a member of the chicory family. The dark burgundy leaves have a strong, bitter flavour; can be cooked or eaten raw in salads.
rocket also known as arugula, rugula and rucola; a peppery-tasting green leaf. Baby rocket leaves (also known as wild rocket) are both smaller and less peppery.

witlof also known as chicory or belgian endive; cigar-shaped with tightly packed heads and pale, yellow-green tips. Has a slight bitter flavour.

Lime pickle an Indian special mixed pickle/condiment of limes that adds a hot and spicy taste to meals, especially rice. Available in Indian food shops.

Malibu coconut-flavoured rum.

Mandarin small, loose-skinned citrus fruit also known as tangerine. Segments in a light syrup are available canned.

Mango tropical fruit with skin colour ranging from green through yellow to deep red. Fragrant deep-yellow flesh surrounds a large flat seed. Mango cheeks in a light syrup are available canned.
green sour and crunchy green mangoes are just immature fruit. Often available from Asian grocery stores.

Maple syrup a thin syrup distilled from the sap of the maple tree. Maple-flavoured syrup or pancake syrup is not an adequate substitute for the real thing.

Marjoram an aromatic herb that is a member of the mint family; has long, thin, oval-shaped, pale-green leaves and a sweet taste similar to oregano. Used fresh or dried.

Marmalade a preserve based on citrus fruit and its rind; cooked with sugar until the mixture has an intense flavour and thick consistency.

Mascarpone *see cheese.*

Mayonnaise a rich, creamy dressing made with egg yolks, vegetable oil, mustard and vinegar or lemon juice. We prefer to use whole egg mayonnaise in our recipes.

Mince also known as ground meat, as in beef, veal, lamb, pork and chicken.

Mirin a champagne-coloured cooking wine from Japan; made of glutinous rice and alcohol and used only for cooking. Do not confuse with drinking sake.

Mushrooms
button small, cultivated white mushrooms with a mild flavour.
enoki clumps of long, spaghetti-like stems with tiny, snowy-white caps.
flat large, flat mushrooms with a rich, earthy flavour. Are sometimes misnamed field mushrooms, which are wild mushrooms.
oyster also known as abalone; grey-white mushroom shaped like a fan. Prized for their smooth texture and subtle, oyster-like flavour.
shiitake when fresh are also known as chinese black, forest or golden oak mushrooms; although cultivated, they have the earthiness and taste of wild mushrooms. Are large and meaty. When dried, they are also known as donko or dried chinese mushrooms; rehydrate before use.
swiss brown also known as cremini or roman mushrooms; are light brown mushrooms having a full-bodied flavour. Button or cup mushrooms can be substituted.

Mustard
american-style bright yellow in colour; a sweet mustard made from mustard seeds, sugar, salt, spices and garlic.
dijon a pale brown, fairly mild french mustard.
powder finely ground white (yellow) mustard seeds.
seeds, yellow also known as white mustard seeds; used ground for mustard powder and in most prepared mustards.

wholegrain also known as seeded. A french-style coarse-grain mustard made from crushed mustard seeds and dijon-style french mustard.

Noodles
fresh rice also known as ho fun, khao pun, sen yau, pho or kway tiau. Can be purchased in strands of various widths or large sheets weighing about 500g, which are then cut into the noodle size required. Chewy and pure white, they do not need pre-cooking before use.
fried crispy egg noodles that have been deep-fried then packaged for sale on supermarket shelves.
rice vermicelli also known as sen mee, mei fun or bee hoon. Made with rice flour. Before using, soak dried noodles in hot water until softened, boil them briefly then rinse with hot water.

Nutmeg the dried nut of an evergreen tree native to Indonesia; it is available in ground form or you can grate your own with a fine grater.

Nuts
almonds flat, pointy-tipped nuts having a pitted brown shell enclosing a creamy white kernel that is covered by a brown skin. *Blanched almonds* have had their brown skins removed. *Almond meal* is also known as ground almonds; nuts are powdered to a coarse flour texture for use in baking or as a thickening agent. *Slivered almonds* are small pieces cut lengthways.
cashews a kidney-shaped nut that grows out from the bottom of the cashew apple; have a sweet, buttery flavour. Because of their high fat content, they should be stored, tightly wrapped, in the refrigerator to retard rancidity.

hazelnuts also known as filberts. Plump, grape-size, rich, sweet nut having a brown inedible skin that is removed by rubbing heated nuts together vigorously in a tea-towel. *Hazelnut meal* is made by grounding the hazelnuts into a coarse flour texture for use in baking or as a thickening agent.
pecans a golden-brown, rich, buttery nut.
pine nuts also known as pignoli; not, in fact, a nut but a small, cream-coloured kernel from pine cones.
pistachios delicately flavoured, pale-green nut inside hard off-white shells. To peel, soak shelled nuts in boiling water for about 5 minutes; drain, then pat dry with absorbent paper. Rub skins with cloth to peel.

Oil
cooking spray we use a cholesterol-free cooking spray made from canola oil.
hazelnut pressed from ground hazelnuts.
olive made from ripened olives. Extra virgin and virgin are the first and second press, respectively, and are therefore considered the best; "extra light" or "light"-types refers to taste not fat levels.
peanut pressed from ground peanuts; the most commonly used oil in Asian cooking because of its high smoke point (capacity to handle high heat without burning).
sesame made from roasted, crushed, white sesame seeds; a flavouring rather than a cooking medium.
vegetable sourced from plants rather than animal fats.
walnut pressed from ground walnuts.

Olives
kalamata small, sharp-tasting brine-cured black olives.

green harvested before fully ripened and are, as a rule, denser and more bitter than their black or brown relatives.
niçoise small black olives.

Onions

brown and white are interchangeable. Their pungent flesh adds flavour to a vast range of dishes.
fried sold in Asian grocery stores packed in jars or in cellophane bags. Make your own by cutting onions into paper-thin slices, then deep-frying in peanut oil; drain on absorbent paper before storing in an airtight container.
green also known as scallion or, incorrectly, shallot; an immature onion picked before the bulb has formed, having a long, bright-green edible stalk.
red also known as spanish, red spanish or bermuda onion; a sweet-flavoured, large, purple-red onion.
shallot also called french or golden shallot or eschalot; small, brown-skinned member of the onion family. Grows in tight clusters similar to garlic.

Orecchiette pasta small disc-shaped pasta; translates literally as "little ears".

Oregano a herb having a woody stalk with clumps of tiny, dark green leaves with a pungent, peppery flavour. Can be used fresh or dried; also known as wild marjoram.

Paprika ground dried sweet red capsicum (bell pepper); there are many grades and types available, including sweet, hot, mild and smoked.

Parsley, flat-leaf also known as continental or italian parsley.

Passionfruit also known as granadilla; a small tropical fruit, comprised of a tough outer skin surrounding edible black sweet-sour seeds.

Peanut butter peanuts ground to a paste; available in both crunchy and smooth varieties.

Pepitas dried pumpkin seeds.

Peppercorns

black the berry clusters are plucked when not quite ripe then left to ferment then dry in the sun until they are shrivelled and nearly black.
green soft, unripe berry of the pepper plant; usually sold packed in brine (occasionally found dried, packed in salt). Has a fresher flavour and less pungency than black pepper.
pink not actually a member of the pepper family although it is often marketed as such; is the dried berry from a type of rose plant grown in Madagascar. Usually sold packed in brine; has a pungently sweet taste.
sichuan peppercorns also known as szechuan or chinese pepper, native to the Sichuan province of China. Small, mildly-hot, red-brown aromatic seeds that resemble black peppercorns; they have a peppery-lemon flavour. Although it is not related to the peppercorn family, the berries look like black peppercorns.
white from the fully ripened berries that are just about to turn red. After harvest the clusters are soaked in water, which softens the outer coating to reveal gray centres. Once dried, they become naturally bleached to white.

Pepper medley a mixture of black, white, green and pink peppercorns, coriander seeds and allspice; sold in disposable grinders in supermarkets. You can make your own blend using various peppercorns.

Pepperoni a spicy variety of dry salami usually made of pork and beef, although other meats can be used, and heavily seasoned with spices.

Polenta also known as cornmeal; a flour-like cereal made of dried corn (maize); sold ground in different textures. Also the name of the dish made from it.

Pomegranate native to the Middle East; a dark-red, leathery-skinned fresh fruit about the size of a large orange. Each fruit is filled with hundreds of seeds, each wrapped in an edible lucent-crimson pulp having a unique tangy sweet-sour flavour.

Pork

butterflied steak boneless mid-loin chop, split in half and flattened.
cutlet sirloin cutlets are boneless thin cuts of meat from the loin; leg cutlets are cut from the middle of the leg.
fillet boneless eye-fillet cut from the loin. It is one of the most tender cuts of pork.
loin chop tender, prime chops with a characteristic T-bone on one side.
medallions pork fillet sliced crosswise and opened out.
neck sometimes called pork scotch; cut from the foreloin without any bones.
pancetta an Italian unsmoked bacon; pork belly that is cured in salt and spices then rolled into a sausage shape and dried for several weeks.
prosciutto cured, air-dried (unsmoked), pressed ham.
shoulder joint sold with bone in or out.
spareribs long cut from the lower portion of the pig, and includes up to 13 long bones.

Potato

baby new also known as chats; not a separate variety but an early harvest with very thin skin.
kipfler small, finger-shaped potato with a nutty flavour.

Poultry

chicken, barbecued a shop-bought whole barbecued chicken weighing about 900g.
chicken breast fillet breast halved, skinned and boned.
chicken drumette small fleshy part of the wing between shoulder and elbow, trimmed to resemble a drumstick.
chicken drumstick leg with skin and bone intact.
chicken maryland leg and thigh still connected in a single piece; bones and skin intact.
chicken, small also known as spatchcock (poussin), no more than 6 weeks old, weighing a maximum of 500g.
chicken thigh skin and thigh bone intact.
chicken thigh fillet thigh with skin and centre bone removed.
chicken wing the whole wing, bone and skin intact.
duck maryland thigh and drumstick still connected; skin still on.
quail small, delicate-flavoured game birds ranging in weight from 250g to 300g; also known as partridge.
turkey breast fillet breast halved, skinned and boned.

Preserved lemon a North African specialty; lemons are quartered and preserved in salt, lemon juice and water. To use, remove and discard pulp, squeeze juice from rind; rinse rind well then slice thinly. Sold in jars or singly by delicatessens; once opened, store under refrigeration.

Quinoa (keen-wa) the seed of a leafy plant similar to spinach. Is gluten-free and thought to be safe for consumption by people with coeliac disease. Has cooking qualities similar to rice, and a delicate, slightly nutty taste. Available from most health-food stores and some delicatessens. Keep sealed in a glass jar under refrigeration as it spoils easily.

Taco seasoning mix found in most supermarkets; is meant to duplicate the taste of a Mexican sauce made from oregano, cumin, chillies and other spices.

Tahini a rich sesame-seed paste available from Middle-Eastern grocery stores and health-food shops; often used in hummus, baba ghanoush and other Lebanese recipes.

Tamarind concentrate the commercial distillation of tamarind pulp into a condensed paste. Thick and purple-black, it is ready-to-use, with no soaking or straining required; can be diluted with water according to taste. Found in Asian supermarkets.

Tarragon an aromatic herb with dark green leaves and an anise-like flavour.

Thyme a member of the mint family; there are many types of this herb but we most often use the "household" variety known as french thyme, or simply called thyme in most shops. It has tiny grey-green leaves that give off a pungent minty, light-lemon aroma.

Tofu also known as bean curd; an off-white, custard-like product made from the "milk" of crushed soya beans. Comes fresh as soft or firm, and processed as fried or pressed dried sheets. Leftover fresh tofu can be refrigerated in water (which is changed daily) for up to four days.

Tomatoes
cherry also known as tiny tim or tom thumb tomatoes; small, round tomatoes.

egg also called plum or roma, these are smallish, oval-shaped tomatoes.
grape small, long oval-shaped tomatoes with a good flavour.
pasta sauce a prepared tomato-based sauce (sometimes called ragu or sugo on the label); comes in varying degrees of thickness and with different flavourings.
paste triple-concentrated tomato puree.
semi-dried partially dried tomato pieces in olive oil; softer and juicier than sun-dried, these are not preserved thus do not keep as long as sun-dried.
sun-dried in oil tomato pieces that have been dried with salt; this dehydrates the tomato and concentrates the flavour. We use sun-dried tomatoes packaged in oil, unless otherwise specified.
sun-dried tomato pesto a thick paste made from sun-dried tomatoes, oil, vinegar and herbs.
truss also known as vine-ripened tomatoes. Small vine-ripened tomatoes with the vine still attached.

Triple sec a strong, clear orange-flavoured liqueur. Curaçao, Cointreau, and Grand Marnier are all triple secs.

Turmeric available fresh and ground. Fresh is also known as kamin; is a rhizome related to galangal and ginger. Must be grated or pounded to release its somewhat acrid aroma and pungent flavour.

Vanilla extract obtained from vanilla beans infused in water.

Veal
cutlets a small cut of meat, usually from the leg or ribs.
loin chops cut from the loin section.
fillet also known as tenderloin; a long, boneless cut of meat from the loin.

Vietnamese mint not a mint at all, but a pungent and peppery narrow-leafed member of the buckwheat family; also called cambodian mint or laksa leaf.

Vine leaves also known as grapevine leaves. Packed in brine in cryovac-packs and can be found in most Middle-Eastern grocery stores.

Vinegar
balsamic there are many balsamic vinegars on the market ranging in pungency and quality depending on how, and for how long, they have been aged. It is a deep rich brown colour with a sweet and sour flavour. Quality can be determined up to a point by price; use the most expensive sparingly.
cider also known as apple cider vinegar; made from fermented apples.
raspberry made from fresh raspberries steeped in a white wine vinegar.
red wine made from red wine.
rice a colourless vinegar made from fermented rice and flavoured with sugar and salt. Also known as seasoned rice vinegar; sherry can be substituted.
white made from spirit of cane sugar.
white wine made from white wine.

Vodka originally a local spirit made from whatever surplus grain or starch-based material (potato) was available. It is now produced almost entirely from grains (usually barley, wheat or rye).

Wasabi a pungent, green-coloured horseradish accompaniment; sold in powdered or paste form.

Water chestnut resemble true chestnuts in appearance, hence the English name. Small brown tubers with a crisp, white, nutty-tasting flesh. Best experienced fresh; however, canned water chestnuts are more easily obtained and can be kept for about a month in the refrigerator, once opened.

Watercress one of the cress family, a large group of peppery greens. Highly perishable, so it must be used as soon as possible after purchase.

Wombok also known as peking cabbage, chinese cabbage or petsai. Elongated in shape with pale green, crinkly leaves, this is the most common cabbage in South-East Asian cooking.

Yeast a raising agent used in dough making.

Za'atar a blend of whole roasted sesame seeds, sumac and crushed dried herbs. Available from spice shops and Middle-Eastern food stores.

Zucchini also known as courgette; small, pale- or dark-green, yellow or white vegetable belonging to the squash family. Its young flowers are also edible.

conversion chart

MEASURES

One Australian metric measuring cup holds approximately 250ml; one Australian metric tablespoon holds 20ml; one Australian metric teaspoon holds 5ml.

The difference between one country's measuring cups and another's is within a two- or three-teaspoon variance, and will not affect your cooking results. North America, New Zealand and the United Kingdom use a 15ml tablespoon.

All cup and spoon measurements are level. The most accurate way of measuring dry ingredients is to weigh them. When measuring liquids, use a clear glass or plastic jug with the metric markings.

We use large eggs with an average weight of 60g.

DRY MEASURES

metric	imperial
15g	½oz
30g	1oz
60g	2oz
90g	3oz
125g	4oz (¼lb)
155g	5oz
185g	6oz
220g	7oz
250g	8oz (½lb)
280g	9oz
315g	10oz
345g	11oz
375g	12oz (¾lb)
410g	13oz
440g	14oz
470g	15oz
500g	16oz (1lb)
750g	24oz (1½lb)
1kg	32oz (2lb)

LIQUID MEASURES

metric	imperial
30ml	1 fluid oz
60ml	2 fluid oz
100ml	3 fluid oz
125ml	4 fluid oz
150ml	5 fluid oz (¼ pint/1 gill)
190ml	6 fluid oz
250ml	8 fluid oz
300ml	10 fluid oz (½ pint)
500ml	16 fluid oz
600ml	20 fluid oz (1 pint)
1000ml (1 litre)	1¾ pints

LENGTH MEASURES

metric	imperial
3mm	⅛in
6mm	¼in
1cm	½in
2cm	¾in
2.5cm	1in
5cm	2in
6cm	2½in
8cm	3in
10cm	4in
13cm	5in
15cm	6in
18cm	7in
20cm	8in
23cm	9in
25cm	10in
28cm	11in
30cm	12in (1ft)

OVEN TEMPERATURES

These oven temperatures are only a guide for conventional ovens. For fan-forced ovens, check the manufacturer's manual.

	°C (Celsius)	°F (Fahrenheit)	Gas Mark
Very slow	120	250	½
Slow	150	275-300	1-2
Moderately slow	160	325	3
Moderate	180	350-375	4-5
Moderately hot	200	400	6
Hot	220	425-450	7-8
Very hot	240	475	9

First published in 2008 by ACP Books, Sydney
Reprinted 2010.
ACP Books are published by ACP Magazines,
a division of PBL Media Pty Limited

ACP Books
General manager *Christine Whiston*
Editor-in-chief *Susan Tomnay*
Creative director & designer *Hieu Chi Nguyen*
Senior editor *Wendy Bryant*
Food director *Pamela Clark*
Food editor *Louise Patniotis*
Additional writing *Alexandra Somerville*
Nutritional information *Belinda Farlow*
Sales & rights director *Brian Cearnes*
Marketing manager *Bridget Cody*
Senior business analyst *Rebecca Varela*
Operations manager *David Scotto*
Production manager *Victoria Jefferys*

Published by ACP Books, a division of ACP Magazines Ltd.
54 Park St, Sydney NSW Australia 2000.
GPO Box 4088, Sydney, NSW. 2001.
Phone +61 2 9282 8618 Fax +61 2 9267 9438
acpbooks@acpmagazines.com.au
www.acpbooks.com.au

To order books,
phone 136 116 (within Australia) or
order online at www.acpbooks.com.au
Send recipe enquiries to:
receipeenquiries@acpmagazines.com.au

Printed by Toppan Printing Co., in China.

Australia Distributed by Network Services, GPO Box 4088, Sydney, NSW 2001.
Phone +61 2 9282 8777 Fax +61 2 9264 3278
networkweb@networkservicescompany.com.au
United Kingdom Distributed by Australian Consolidated Press (UK),
10 Scirocco Close, Moulton Park Office Village, Northampton, NN3 6AP.
Phone +44 1604 642 200 Fax +44 1604 642 300
books@acpuk.com www.acpuk.com
New Zealand Distributed by Southern Publishers Group, 21 Newton Road, Auckland.
Phone +64 9 360 0692 Fax +64 9 360 0695 hub@spg.co.nz
South Africa Distributed by PSD Promotions, 30 Diesel Road Isando, Gauteng Johannesburg.
PO Box 1175, Isando 1600, Gauteng Johannesburg.
Phone +27 11 392 6065/6/7 Fax +27 11 392 6079/80 orders@psdprom.co.za
Canada Distributed by Publishers Group Canada
Order Desk & Customer Service 9050 Shaughnessy Street, Vancouver, BC V6P 6E5
Phone (800) 663 5714 Fax (800) 565 3770 service@raincoast.com

Title: Barbecue: the Australian women's weekly / compiler, Pamela Clark.
Publisher: Sydney : ACP Books, 2008.
ISBN: 978-1-86396-791-4 (pbk.)
Notes: Includes index.
Subjects: Barbecue cookery.
Other Authors/Contributors: Clark, Pamela
Dewey Number: 641.5784
© ACP Magazines Ltd 2008
ABN 18 053 273 546

Cover photographer *Dean Wilmot*
Cover stylist *Kate Nixon*
Special feature photographer *George Seper*
Special feature stylist *Kate Nixon*
Special feature food preparation *Ariarne Bradshaw*

Photographers *Alan Benson, Andrew Young, Ashley Mackevicius, Brett Stevens, Ian Wallace,
Joshua Dasey, Luke Burgess, Steve Brown, Tanya Zouev*
Stylists *Amber Keller, David Morgan, Jane Hann, Julz Beresford, Justine Osborne, Kate Murdoch,
Louise Pickford, Margot Braddon, Marie-Helene Clauzon, Mary Harris, Michaela le Compte,
Sarah O'Brien, Trish Heagerty*

The publishers would like to thank Anthony and Kerry Freeman and John and Jeannette
Lambert, also Barbeques Galore, Duck Egg Blue, Hart & Heim, Howards Storage World,
Jedo's Beach House, My Island Home, Outliving; Spence & Lyda, Sunny Lifestyle, The Bay
Tree, The Essential Ingredient, Until, Yardgames.